25 EASY STEPS TO PEOPLE MANAGEMENT

Duncan Andrews

© Copyright Duncan Andrews 2018

Thanks for buying 25 Easy Steps To People Management. The book is a "How to" or "Step-by-step" guide on providing over 25 daily, weekly or monthly tasks. Most of the 25 subjects have an accompanying template (in Microsoft Office format) to help deliver the task. Also included are templates to allow the manager to make self-assessments of how they are doing. All these results can be entered into a manager's dashboard template to see their overall success rate. There are 26 templates in total.

Download them at www.duncanjandrews.co.uk

Duncan Andrews

duncanjandrews@hotmail.com

CONTENTS

Introduction	7
Good Behaviours	15
Bad Behaviours	24
Step 1 - Choose the Right Team	29
Step 2 - Define Responsibilities	39
Step 3 - Job Descriptions	43
Step 4 - Are Your 1:1s Really Just 0:1s?	48
Step 5 - Yearly Appraisals	52
Step 6 - Department Meeting	58
Step 7 - Delegation	63
Step 8 - Goal Setting	74
Step 9 - Staff Development	80
Step 10 - Coaching	87
Step 11 - Converting Company Goals Into Actions	100
Step 12 - Retain Your Staff	105
Step 13 - Brainstorming	108
Step 14 - Quarterly Plans	113
Step 15 - Empower Your Staff	121
Step 16 - Fully Exploit Your Staff Skills	125
Step 17 - Skills Matrix	129
Step 18 - Staff Logbooks	136
Step 19 - Teambuilding (Without Oil Drums and Planks)	140
Step 20 - Job Swapping	143
Step 21 - 360° Degree Reviews	148
Step 22 - Balancing Workloads	159
Step 23 - Reverse Feedback	164

Step 24 - Difficult Conversations Made Easier ... 172
Step 25 - Troublesome Staff ... 178
Step 25 - Still Got Troublesome Staff? ... 179
Manager's Dashboard ... 184
Micro Manager or Disengaged Star Gazer? ... 187
How Approachable is Your Department? ... 192
A List of The Templates ... 194

INTRODUCTION

Blah-blah-blah and crocheting. Yes this is a management book – I'd better explain.

Imagine you went for your first flying lesson and the only instruction you were given was to "be one with the plane". You would run a mile from your flight instructor (well, you should - and the instructor is probably a plumber). If you are one of those insane adrenalin junkies, you may have decided to stay but would be left wondering about thrust, drag, stall speeds, climb rates and pre-flight checks. When learning to fly, you need more than a "motivational" saying to get off the ground and land without killing yourself. By mastering all the sub-tasks (the deliverables) you should attain your goal of safe, happy flying. It's the same with management (and certainly safer).

While doing the research for this book, I posted a question to a number of management groups on LinkedIn. I specifically asked for real world, anecdotal, examples of good management "in practice". I expressly stated that I didn't want any leadership soundbites that you see on motivational posters, such as "Lead by Example"; "Build Trust" or "Respect is Something Earned". My post received over 300 comments, which is pretty good for LinkedIn. All but 2 of the responses were lifted straight from the motivational quotes I specifically didn't want. I realised that people couldn't get away from cool soundbites. Blah-blah-blah.

I accept that there was the factor of self-promotion affecting the quality of the responses. LinkedIn encourages group involvement so people can write anything to show they have been engaged. Most of the people who responded to my post, would have been just as helpful if they had listed a load of vegetables.

Two respondents took the time and effort to write a proper reply, but they weren't particularly good examples of management behaviour, so maybe a vegetable would have done a better job there too.

Crocheting. Management books are boring right? I've started a few and finished none. So what better way to break up the monotony by adding in some bad puns about a subject I know nothing about. A comedian once said that a pun is the lowest form of wit and should really stand for "punch him in the mouth", but please don't – I value my crooked yellow ones – they are all I have. Crocheting was an entirely random choice, so don't expect to learn anything (I didn't) – I just needed a vehicle to help "hook" you in. (There is your first bad wordplay. I can't guarantee I won't use that one again – there is a limit to what you can do with crocheting. Scarf anyone?)

There is also another running theme that I will let you discover for yourself. This is not a book of jokes or a joke book. The puns and wordplay are just there to lighten the mood, but make no mistake my message is serious.

What right do I have to write a management book?

Over the years I have managed people while working in small and large companies. I also ran my own business for 8 years employing 5 people. On the flip side, I have had some really terrible bosses who had less empathy with people than my goldfish.

I realised that over these 25 years, I have been observing good and bad managers and the impact they have on people. One interesting point is that the bad managers had a bigger impact on me than the good ones – people always remember the bad guy!

My justifications to write a book are:

- I regularly got significantly higher ratings as a manager than my counterparts in annual employee surveys while I worked for a large multi-national.

- When attending management/leadership courses, I didn't learn many new techniques because I was doing them already. Techniques that some of my fellow attendees regarded as revolutionary "blue sky" thinking, I was already doing because, to me, they were common sense. When the idea of a "1:1" is regarded as mind-blowing then there are some serious questions to ask. Maybe this is a confirmation of how bad they were as managers rather than a statement of how good I was.

- Maintained extremely high staff retention over the years. 100% over 9 years while working for the multi-national company.

- Look at the recommendations from my previous staff members on my LinkedIn profile. https://uk.linkedin.com/in/duncanandrews

Over the years, I have attended some "leadership" courses – some were good and some were very bad.

On one bad course, the trainers spent all their time trying to catch us out and showing what bad managers we were by playing games that could only end in failure. There was no positive reinforcement at all. All of the attendees finished the course having learnt nothing useful at all. When we were leaving there was a lot of mumbling along the lines of "what a waste of my time and company money".

A Good course. Organised by the same company who had organised the bad course above – they must have received some bad feedback from the first one. The tone and ethos of this course was completely opposite to the first one. It focused on the daily, weekly, monthly and yearly tasks that a manager should be providing for their staff. I came away with 2 interesting observations:

- I was already doing 90% of what they taught, which gave me the thumbs up that I was doing the right things. To me, these regular deliverables seemed like common sense.

- A large number of managers above me in the organisation (Directors and Vice Presidents) who learnt a lot from this course. Obviously they hadn't regarded these tasks as common sense (more like rocket science) and had never delivered some of the most basic "people management" tasks like 1:1s and department meetings. Through the course exercises and breakout sessions I learnt that a lot of these bad pennies displayed the following behaviours:

- No regular 1:1s

- No department meetings (I couldn't believe this when I first heard it. To me, this is one of the most basic functions of a department. How can people be expected to work together if they never meet as a group?)

- No team building or coaching.

- Using yearly appraisals to drop nasty surprises onto unsuspecting staff.

- No development or training.

- A lack of inclusion – the manager wasn't asking for any input from the team. What a loss of brain power.

- Rife favouritism – the boss giving their close mate the best of everything whether they earned it or not (usually not).

- A complete lack of understanding of people and how they tick.

To be fair to these bad managers, it was clear that this was their first leadership course in their life, so I couldn't lay the blame squarely at their feet for their lack of abilities. It is unusual for organisations to commit to high quality management training, so there is no surprise that I have encountered so many poor managers. It is a credit to the company that I worked for that they decided to expend some real time and money into improving the quality of their leaders.

To be honest, I finished the course with mixed feelings – A positive affirmation that I had been doing the right things and a slight disgruntlement that quite a lot of people, who had higher positions than me, hadn't got a clue about managing people. But that's life I suppose.

Even with the best training in the world, there are some people who are so lacking in empathy, that no amount of training will make them good managers. Their staff would be better off trying to forge a relationship with a jellyfish.

Routes Into Management

You will see me carping on about bad managers in this book – partly to let off steam but mainly to demonstrate the effects of bad management behaviours. However, these poor managers are not entirely to blame as there a number of root causes, one of which is the route into management – ie How did they get to become a manager? It is worth quickly reviewing some of the routes into management as it puts some behaviours into context:

- Longest Serving Employee. Sometimes, when the manager's role becomes available, the longest serving team member gets the job. This presents them with a whole set of new challenges mainly focused around the relationships they have with people who used to be their equals (and mates). Everyone struggles with how the new relationship should work. The fact that the company has given the job to the longest serving employee also suggests they have been lazy (no time consuming recruitment process) and will continue this theme by providing no management training. The new boss very often struggles with the personal relationships because they are torn between being a manager and a mate and fails to gain the necessary command over the team. Sadly, it is common for these new managers to be unhappy and fail resulting in them leaving the company or requesting to be put back into the team.

- Specialist. Regardless of the products a company produces there will be specialists who have taken years to acquire all their knowledge, whether it be about baking fairy cakes or designing car engines. Specialists are usually well paid, command respect and enjoy being the "go to" person for technical queries – they are usually, therefore, happy and satisfied in their role. When they become the manager, they no longer have time to do their "specialisation thing" as they have to devote a large portion of their time to managerial work or they do the opposite and carry on being the specialist, ignoring their managerial duties. Both scenarios result in dissatisfaction for both the new manager and the team. I have seen a number of specialists, after having been managers for a few months, request that a new manager is recruited, so they can go back to being a specialist again. I'm generalising, but most specialists don't make good managers and should be left to get on with what they are good at (this is also good for the company).

- The right place at the wrong time. Some people gain management roles who are relatively new to the organisation and are not very knowledgeable either. Initially, they will feel they were in the right place at the right time but results will show they were not ready, so it will turn out to be the wrong time. These individuals are usually keen to do a good job, so will be open minded and receptive to learning although the curve is steep.

- The right place at the right time. Sometimes the timing is just right for someone with enough experience to move up the chain of command. Typically these individuals will take their new role seriously and will want to deliver the best possible experience to their staff. I have been in this position once.

What Does This Book Give You?

To gain the respect and trust of your team, you need to deliver to your staff on a daily, weekly, monthly and annual basis.

You can attain all those high-level relationships (such as trust and respect) by delivering the regular sub-tasks - for example 1:1s, department meetings, coaching, fair appraisals etc. If you provide these duties professionally then you will automatically acquire the trust and respect.

The additional benefit is that your team will deliver more effectively because you will have empowered them to get on with the job without your interference. Trust and respect are a two way thing. If you respect and trust your employees, they will reciprocate and you don't need to micro-manage the output they produce.

This book focuses on the management of people instead of general management techniques, but by focusing on the managing of your people you will have a team that is efficient; productive and satisfied.

Manage People to Success!

Most of the chapters in this book fit broadly into one of two categories:

- Essentials. These are the regular tasks that you MUST deliver in order to be a good manager.

- Making the most of your team. As it suggests, these are the techniques that, if utilised, will transform your team into a productive; efficient; contributory; satisfied unit.

There are 25 free templates included to provide a means of recording the results of your staff and, just as importantly, yourself. A high number of the templates are designed for your self-analysis of your performance. There is a computer term "Garbage In: Garbage Out" – so if you feed rubbish in, then you will only get rubbish out. The same applies to your self-analysis templates – you have to be truthful and pragmatic with your entries. If you use the templates wisely, they will provide realistic appraisals of where you are currently and what you should focus on. There is one template called the Manager's Dashboard, in which you can enter all the results from the other templates and it will display how well you are performing overall.

If you are reading this while in the book shop and have no intention of buying me, then head straight to the chapters called "Bad Behaviours" and "Good Behaviours" as they will give you a quick precis on management behaviours while you wife buys those shoes/husband buys a quadcopter. (Choose accordingly).

GOOD BEHAVIOURS

Here is a summary of good management behaviours, in no particular order:

Clear Decision Making. This was one of the earliest lessons taught to me by a staff member. In my early days, I was trying to manage by consensus and keep everyone happy which resulted in decisions being delayed and some confusion amongst the team. I was told by one of my team that they expected me to make clear decisions. One caveat to remember is that clear decision making does NOT mean that you are always right. Be prepared to alter your decision if the situation changes – there is no value in doggedly sticking to your first decision if it transpires it was the wrong one. Clearly, repeatedly changing your decision is not good for your reputation either so it is important to try and make the correct decision first time by thoroughly exploring all the relevant parameters.

Consistency. Multiple aspects of your behaviour should be consistent to earn the trust of your team, to include:

- Decision Making
- The hours you do
- 1:1 and Appraisal Feedback
- Delegation
- Communication

You know what, it's easier to list the items where you don't need to be consistent:

No Favouritism. We all like some people more than others and that is fine and normal but as a manager, you can't let your personal preferences translate into actions. Everyone deserves the same level of (consistent) behaviour from their manager. If you start giving better equipment (iPhone6 rather than iPhone5); awarding bonuses and providing improved development opportunities to the people you like, then that is clear favouritism. It will get noticed and your team will lose trust in you.

Stand Up For your Team (Most of the Time). Your employees are entitled to be treated professionally and courteously. There will be times when people from other departments (including customers) are rude and unprofessional in their behaviour. Part of your role is to act as the firewall for your department – i.e. you are there to safeguard against unwarranted attacks. Your team needs to see that you will stand up for them when justified. Some folks get away with discourteous behaviour regularly (through inflated ego or false belief that their title gives them the validation to do so). Through experience, I know that most of these types are paper tigers – stand up to them once and they will be Snow White from then on. Let the other departments accept their poor conduct, but not yours.

Conversely there will be times when it would be a mistake to defend one of your team if they have behaved unprofessionally or in a derogatory manner. As an adult, they are answerable for their actions and it is not your responsibility to resolve all their, self-made, problems. In a case like this, you should talk to your employee and reinforce the accepted behaviours you expect to see and also stress that they are accountable for their actions. It is their obligation to contact the other person to apologise and resolve how to work together in the future. Equally important is to contact the other person to tell them that the matter has been dealt with and to expect some communication from your (naughty) team member.

Walk the Walk – don't just say it – DO IT. Walking the walk means delivering on your managerial promises and behaviours. Lots of (bad) managers talk a good talk about how they manager their people, but don't actually deliver. And of course, the really bad managers, can't even talk the talk; have less empathy that my little toe, are not interested in changing and to be honest, should not be managers at all. What amazes me is the number of people who fall into this last category.

Walking the walk does take effort and sometimes it will seem like a bind to make time for an employee to do yet another, good quality 1:1, but the ramifications of letting things slip are negative and long lasting, so it really does pay off to make that special effort.

Treat People Like Adults. In all aspects of their working life, people will try to grow; mature and remain professional. This should be at the forefront of the manager's mind when dealing with people privately, but even more significantly, in a group. There will be times when you get frustrated or annoyed by someone's behaviour and you are tempted to deliver a good chiding. Apart from making you feel better (for about a minute), the negative fallout from this is widespread and long lasting. People cannot be made to feel like they are being told off by a teacher or parent as this is demeaning; demoralising and is ultimately bad for the bottom line. All of your communications should be respectful and courteous without a demeaning undertone, even if you have to deliver bad news or criticise someone for poor performance or bad behaviours.

Parent:Child Relationships. Although this appears to be similar to "Treat People Like Adults", it is in fact completely different. The principle is that if you treat someone like a child they will act like one. If you demonstrate parental tendencies towards your staff, they will tend to expect it and act accordingly. It can best be demonstrated in two ways:

1. People come to you and expect solutions on a plate. You employ responsible individuals to deliver and they have to use all their personal resources to do so. If you get into the habit of delivering results for people, they will stop trying for themselves. It is acceptable, indeed beneficial, if you are involved in helping

to solve a difficult problem, but for normal deliverables your staff need to do this for themselves. If you are approached for the "quick solution", encourage your staff member to go looking for the solution for themselves – it is more rewarding and they are less likely to come back in future for the quick resolution.

2. You expect people to act in a "grown up" way. We are all human and intermittently there will be some personal issues between staff members for a variety of root causes. There is a strong chance they will turn to you for arbitration. (Actually, they will both be independently expecting you to side with them.) I got caught out by this situation a number of times until I realised that these people needed to sort the problem out themselves in a professional and courteous manner. Your job is to simply state that you expect a resolution to the issue by (set a date) and in a professional and respectful manner. This may fail. You have given them the opportunity to act maturely and they have let you down. Now you can step up the narrative and state that they have let you down, but you will now act as arbitrator and that you expect all future issues to be resolved maturely and professionally or there will be consequences.

Look Inwards – Most of the Time. Your department has something to deliver and your team are the ones to do that (not you – definitely not you), so it makes sense to spend most of your time looking into the department. Part of your responsibility is to understand and coordinate with the rest of the business, so you clearly need to spend some time looking outwards, but this should not take up the majority.

Don't Micro Manage. You should select a team that has the ability to get on with the work and deliver to accepted standards without the need for someone to continuously look over their shoulders, or worse, intervene. Micro managing isn't really managing at all – it's interfering!

Select the right people; define their roles; set targets and goals (and then appraise, of course) and step back. People will develop; grow; improve with a net result that is greater than the constituent parts.

Don't Gossip. Trust is one of the vital ingredients of the relationship with your staff. If you gossip, the trust will be in the waste bin. Team members will gossip "at you" so be like a one-way valve – flotsam can go in, but nothing must come out. It's a natural human pastime to gossip, but you have to remain tight lipped and hence slightly boring. It's a small price to pay.

Be Realistic. Nobody can give 110%. Very few people live for work – most work to live. Your staff member's personal lives are more important to them than the job. Don't believe me? Ask yourself "Would you sacrifice your family or your job first?" Nine times out of ten, the answer is the job. Accept that people will need to see "Little Josie" in her school play; get sick; get drunk; feel tired or just have a bad day. Realistically you can expect to receive 70-80% commitment on a regular basis. Embrace this state of affairs rather than working against it by making allowances for your team's lives.

Be Bothered. You team delivers all the useful deliverables of your department (or they should be) so it is very important to be bothered about delivering the best managerial experience you can. At a minimum, these are the essentials like good quality 1:1s; regular department meetings; achievable but challenging goals; high quality appraisals. You cannot afford to miss any of these because:

- You are tired

- You go on holiday

- Had too much to drink last night

- Other meeting requests come in

- Staff go on holiday, are sick or had too much to drink last night.

Schedule around these events to ensure they are always delivered.

Don't Be Too Bothered. Some individuals will legitimately require more time with you – perhaps you can see the potential in someone, but they need development or someone is having issues that are worth solving (by them, with your help). People are people, and some will want attention that strictly speaking, is just that. There are no hard and fast rules on this, so you have to assess whether the level of attention they seek is justifiable in terms of your limited time. Folks should be allowed to come and talk to you as an approachable boss but be careful not to be drawn into focusing on individuals who pine for regular limelight.

Communicate Proply! If a team member asks "Boss, should we buy that lot of grey yarn on special offer?", then you cannot answer "The strength of the Pound will depend on the US interest rate". What does that mean? Make sure you answer the question with a definitive answer (if you can). If you don't know the answer, then say so and promise to come back to them later. Ambiguity is the killer of productivity. The communication channel that I have seen that promotes the highest ambiguity is email, so pay particular attention when replying to emails. You should:

- Ensure you answer all questions (if you can). If you cannot answer a question, then promise to look into it and come back to the person. Make sure you do.

- If a question requires a simple or yes/no answer, then take care to provide the relevant response. There is nothing worse than leaving someone hanging with a grey ambiguous answer.

- Be bothered (again) to write wordy responses if the question warrants it. It is time consuming, but you cannot afford to leave people without a direction.

Observe Always. Think of yourself as an omnipresent walking CCTV/Dictaphone. Everything your staff do is an opportunity for you to look for behaviours (good and bad); potential; undeveloped talent etc. You will notice some negative aspects but try to be "glass half full" about it and look for positive traits. If you do spot something negative, then I would not advise approaching someone and stating that "On the 23rd January, at 1:30pm, you spoke to Eric and blah blah blah". This conveys the impression of big brother. Address the situation by all means but don't give away that you are constantly observing, in fact it is wise to never give this away because people will stop acting naturally.

Do the hours. I believe in working smart, so I would not endorse working 14 hours a day to demonstrate how committed you are. However, working from home every Friday and Monday is not a good idea either – your staff expect you to have the same level of commitment as them, so either work 5 days a week, or give them Mondays and Fridays off too (Oops, did I say give them the days off – Freudian slip there – I meant work from home!).

Take on the Paperwork. Admin is slightly less boring than reading a management book (I'm not a natural salesman!). Make sure you do your fair share – your team are not there as a big pool of personal assistants. Whenever I took my team out socialising or on a team-building exercise, I always made sure I used my company credit card to pay, knowing that I would have to process the expenses.

Put Yourself Second. Adopting a general position of putting the team first will be appreciated. The Manager title is just that – you just have a different role than the rest of the team, that's all. Manager does not mean you are first in line for all the finer aspects of working life.

Give Credit Where it is Due. If a member of your team produces outstanding work that attracts praise, then ensure that person receives the necessary accolade. Whatever you do, do not take credit for a team member's work.

Lead From The Back. Nurturing the team to follow you does not mean you have to be at the sharp end. In the spirit of personal development, trust and respect, let your team move forward while you drive from the back. (But don't become a back seat driver!).

Inclusion. Your team are talented, intelligent, creative individuals – use them. 2 heads are better than 1. Foster a culture of inclusion and contribution to extract the maximum capability for your department.

Admit Weaknesses. Admitting weaknesses is a strength, although there are many who are too scared to face up to their weaknesses. Individuals (including you) and as a group, there must be flaws that can be reduced or eliminated. Turning a blind eye to weaknesses will uphold a stagnant culture without possibility of improvement. You could organise a brainstorming session to identify weaknesses both as individuals and as a group. Take the lead and admit your own faults first. Be careful this doesn't become a witch hunt with people pointing out other people's drawbacks. Set the rule that each person can only identify weaknesses in themselves and not others.

Act on Reverse Feedback. Many, many managers are too scared to ask for feedback from their staff and this is usually with good reason. So long as the feedback is focused purely on your delivery as a manager and not something personal like your awful comedy jumpers, then you should encourage reverse feedback. As with admitting your weaknesses, how can you improve without feedback? It is less painful than you think and over time, the feedback should be all positive (so long as you adopt everything from this book ☺).

Plan. If you fail to plan, then you are planning to fail. It's not often I regurgitate something from the internet, but this statement is worth it. Without a plan, anarchy rules. The team need to know where they are heading; what the company goals are and how they will get there. You can set plans for 1:1s; team meetings; brainstorming sessions; team building; appraisals; project assessments. Some of these plans can be set out for the entire year ahead and some, due to their nature, will be more flexible in nature.

Set Goals & Appraise. It is not sufficient to only deliver business as usual objectives. Setting short and long-term goals will advance the department. Opportunities for goal setting can come from external sources or cultivated internally. Goals can be set for small tasks; continuous improvement exercises and for large projects (such as organisational changes). There are many vehicles to identify and describe goals - 1:1s, department meetings; company briefings and of course brainstorming. Your team are a brilliant resource for this. Once goals have been identified, then ensure they are SMART goals – ie Specific, Measurable, Attainable, Realistic and Time-bound. Once set, it is imperative they are appraised appropriately according to the plan. Setting and appraising goals is a fundamental requisite of the manager's role.

Quality Delegation. Micro managers can skip this section because you won't understand it. Staff will expect you to delegate so make sure you do without going too far and just offloading everything onto your team. If you have a lot of spare time, then you have probably unfairly dumped your work on others. Good quality delegation is providing work streams of variable interest and quality ensuring a fair share to all. Reviewing and appraising the net effect is essential but you have to give your staff the space to deliver without constant interference.

Say Thank You. An almost effortless way of showing recognition for good work, with an everlasting upbeat after effect. Can be combined with "Good Work" or "Good Job" if you like your Americanisms. Distribute liberally.

BAD BEHAVIOURS

The long-term impact of a bad manager can be greater than that of a good one, so avoid these behaviours at all cost.

Grey Decision Making. These are generally people afraid to make decisions so come up with a cryptic solution that nobody can understand or deliver on. These people spend a lot of time twiddling their thumbs (yes, physically) while they ruminate for a week to decide if they would like milk in their tea. Often, staff members will leave their grey manager's office thinking to themselves "What decision was made there?"; "What do I do now?"; "What does he want?" or "Did he want black tea?"

Inconsistency. On Monday it's ok for Bonnie to take the decisions relating to her work and on Tuesday it's not. People won't know where they stand and will ultimately not make any decisions for fear of the boss' reaction. Progress and productivity are subdued.

Having Strong Favourites. Rewarding Eric with the biggest bonuses, the best equipment and the latest courses just because he is your friend. Depending on the thickness of Eric's skin he may be embarrassed or not, but your staff will notice and will reciprocate inversely.

Face Outwards. These types spend most of the time looking out from the department (usually upwards because they are constantly thinking of their next promotion). There is a lack of engagement with the team resulting in poor performance and productivity.

Let the Team Defend Themselves. If a difficult situation arises between a team member and somebody from a different department (perhaps a customer), these managers will hide in their office behind a closed door. The team will know that "they are on their own" and can't expect any support from their hermit manager.

Talk the Talk. But don't walk very much. These people have read too many management books and posters and are full of self-importance accompanied with a healthy slice of BS. Regularly, these people are the Outward Facers too. They deliver very little to their staff apart from a good view of the back of their head. Commonly these types also dress very sharply including a shiny pair of long pointy shoes – the length of their shoes is proportionate to their BS quotient.

Treat People Like Children. If you treat people like children, then they will act like children. In all other aspects of their life, these individuals are doing grown up things until their amateurish boss treats them like a child. Manager's who display these behaviours will have a team who struggles to develop and produce because they are constantly demeaned. The manager may feel like he is running a nursery, but the fault is entirely his.

Micro Managing Everything. These managers will look older than their years as a result of doing all the work because micro managers cannot delegate and then not interfere. Employees will be demotivated and will not offer to take on any new work. The department works under a big brother culture, but unfortunately for the staff, there is no diary room.

Keeps All Knowledge in Their Head. In other words, they communicate nothing. Like this……

Rumour Central. To begin with, the manager who spreads gossip can be a fun figure until the staff realise they cannot tell their boss anything in confidence.

David Brent. I'm a big fan of The Office and Ricky Gervais and David Brent is a very well observed character. Being the office entertainer and "best friend" to all may sound appealing but won't result in a very motivated department and the staff will think you are a berk. Just watch The Office to see this in practise.

Expecting 110%. Just not possible – the best you can hope for is 90% on a good day.

My Staff Live For Work. Erm, nooo. The oddity here is that managers who expect staff to live for work, don't themselves. A manager who values their career; family; health; hobbies and education can't expect their staff to abandon all these normal life factors and dedicate themselves to the cause. This behaviour is one of the most significant pointers that the manager has less empathy than a slug.

Can't Be Bothered. When Stan approaches his boss with an issue, in his mind, it is important. Stan won't always come up with issues at a convenient time – it may be when his boss is about to go into a meeting or go to lunch. The "Can't be Bothered" boss will put Stan off to a later date to avoid the disruption to his day. It is not always possible to discuss issues fully if they crop up at inconvenient times, but these manager types can dismiss issues inappropriately. Stan is less likely to talk to his boss going forward. The "Can't Be Bothereds" also let scheduled tasks slide like 1:1s, department meetings, coaching etc resulting in the team not being very bothered either.

Lazy Communication. My observations over the years have shown a direct correlation between a person's seniority and the quality of their communication downwards. As people climb the ladder, their responses to subordinates (particularly by email) get shorter and more "woolly". I have been on the receiving end of this on a number of times – I have asked a question requiring a definite answer and have received 1 or 2 words that don't give me the answer I need. Lazy Communication = Confusion.

Blinkers On. There is nothing to learn by observing team interactions and conduct. These "eyes wide shut" bosses will deliver distorted 1:1s and appraisals because they don't know what's going on. I have seen bosses like this.....but they didn't see me!

Flexi Hours. Arriving last in the office; leaving first and always "working from home" on a Friday. Being the boss doesn't mean you have the right to work a 4 day week, which your staff will assume you are doing. I have been surprised at the number of managers who have taken this approach.

I'm not an Administrator. I once worked for a company where the expenses recording software was very annoying – long winded, not intuitive, repetitive etc. Whenever my boss had credit card expenditure (such as booking training courses; ordering travel tickets or hotels; paying for team building or meals out), she would let her staff use their company credit cards, so they had to go through the pain of using the expenses software.

Me First. Some management advocates believe in leading from the front and that's ok so long as they are still in touch with their team. People cannot follow if the leader is so far in front that they are over the horizon. These managers, typically, reward themselves the best of everything and fail to look over their shoulder to see if the pack is still within arm's reach. It's impossible to lead by example if people can't see the leader.

One Head is Better Than Three. Cerberus didn't think so. This is a non-inclusive approach to management which results in a stale environment with stunted development. Closely aligned with the "blinkers on" type, these managers believe that only they have the intelligence and insight to deliver progress. Just not true.

I Don't Have Any Weaknesses. Nonsense – we all do. These managers will genuinely believe that all faults; mistakes; missed deadlines and over spending are entirely the fault of the staff. They also, commonly, never ask for feedback.

Never Ask For Reverse Feedback. The reason is that these manager types are afraid of what they will hear because, deep down, they know they haven't been delivering. Without feedback, they will never improve.

Extreme Planning. At one end of the spectrum, the team are running around like headless chickens continually putting out fires (mmm, cooked chicken). Very tiring and stressful with little time left over for improvement. It is difficult to understand why any manager would want this scenario, but I have seen it in real life. Maybe they get to step in and solve problems giving them a sense of importance. At the other extreme, there are so many plans in place that people are suffocated with bureaucracy and creativity is extinguished.

Anarchy Rules. Deliver the business as usual objectives and don't set goals for anything else. It's the easy life, achieving the bare minimum. If staff want to take on other work, then let them deal with it themselves – the manager doesn't need to be involved. If they fail, be it on their head. No goal appraisals required. So long as you meet your business as usual KPIs then life is sweet and simple right?

Delegate to Incompetent Staff? No Thanks. Nobody else can provide the skills and quality as the manager – people cannot be trusted. These managers will look like Dorian Gray's portrait as a result of doing everything themselves. They haven't understood that their "Manager" title means they are there to manage people to produce the results. It's not sustainable – they will burn out quicker than a meteorite.

STEP 1 - CHOOSE THE RIGHT TEAM

It is absolutely vital to have the right people in your team, especially if it is a small one. You simply cannot afford to have someone that doesn't fit. The impact is widespread on your team and customers if you have a person that is non-communicative; belligerent; lazy; introspective; rude etc.

In today's business world, everyone has to have a customer culture (including internal customers). In the IT world, historically, you had back-office and customer facing staff. The back-office staff (who were generally the most technically competent) would work on systems in the background and didn't have to face the public or sunlight. They were the "geeks" of the department – pale and intelligent but lacking in personal skills. Over the years, IT systems have become more "human friendly" and don't require a Masters in Physics to switch them on. You could say, the systems have dumbed down although I'm sure some IT professionals would argue against this. Now you don't have to employ the geeks of the old days. Where have they all gone? Do they congregate in disused tunnels to do some hard-core coding? So now there is no clear divide between back-office and customer facing – EVERYONE has to be good with people. Other service departments have evolved in the same way over the years.

It is extremely difficult to change a person's core personality. If you have inherited a "fly in your ointment" person, then good luck because you will struggle. Some coaching and focus can result in minor changes, but you cannot change a leopard's spots.

From my own experiences, I have inherited staff who are more like an elephant in my ointment. I once inherited a guy who was grumpy; non-communicative; didn't follow accepted processes and was anti-customer. I personally witnessed some of our internal customers about to enter our office but quickly changed their mind when they saw my elephant guy at his desk (eating buns). All of your teams' work and all of your efforts to run an efficient, productive department have been "slashed and burned" by this misfit. In the US, the guy (or gal) could be got rid of fairly simply, and by got rid of, I mean sacked, not wearing concrete boots under a new motorway. In Europe, employees have more rights, so you cannot simply dispose of someone (metaphorically) – in fact the process can be complicated and contracted. Thus, choosing the right team in the first place is extremely important – probably one of the most crucial tasks a manager has to do, because if you get it wrong the impact could be long term.

What Does The Business Want?

Every department has it's deliverables – monthly accounts, reliable IT or perfect Third Dimension Crochet Stitches!! (Yes, this is a real stitch). Physicists would say all stitches are in 3 dimensions – it's impossible to produce a 2D stitch from 3D wool. If I see a stitch called Fourth Dimension stitch, then I won't believe it – surely that's only possible with a Tardis?

Putting your department's deliverables aside, what else does the business want? Primarily, it is how does your department behave; how does it interact with others; what is the department's style?

You can try to work this out for yourself, but why do this if the business can tell you? Your stakeholders can provide some invaluable input, so ask them in your scheduled meetings. Done properly this will greatly help with your recruiting process because you can look out for personality traits that will fit the behaviours the business is looking for.

Your stakeholders will need some help to provide useful inputs, so go prepared with some questions. At the same time, get your stakeholders to rate the importance of each. I'll call this the Behaviour Ratings Survey. Reality check – your stakeholders might require a top rating for everything, which is not realistic. Nobody can be good at everything - take me for example – I am a mediocre writer and my puns are not the punniest in the world.

Here is a sample of your questions and rating system:

What Does the Business Want From Your Team?

Category	Trait	Rating 1	2	3	4	5
Communication	Ensures all workers get the pertinent information					
Communication	Communicates company goals to reports/subordinates					
Communication	Can Influence Others					
Communication	Excellent communication skills.					
Communication	Willing to learn and share knowledge.					
Customer Culture	Understands what the customers want (Internal or external)					
Customer Culture	Encourages others to understand customer needs					
Customer Culture	Works well with people in your (client's) organization					
Customer Culture	Is Service minded					
Customer Culture	Is Cooperative					

You should get these ratings from all your stakeholders. If they understand your department, then the ratings should be similar. In the event that they are not, all you can do is take the average by plotting the results in a spreadsheet. See below.

Category	Trait	Accounts	IT	Marketing	Technology	Engineering	Admin	Production	Average
Communication	Ensures all workers get the pertinent information	2	3	3	4	3	5	3	3.3
Communication	Communicates company goals to reports/subordinates	3	2	2	2	3	4	4	2.9
Communication	Can Influence Others	1	1	2	2	1	2	3	1.7
Communication	Excellent communication skills.	4	4	4	3	4	4	3	3.7
Communication	Willing to learn and share knowledge.	5	5	4	4	3	4	5	4.3
Customer Culture	Understands what the customers want (Internal or external)	5	5	5	5	4	5	5	4.9
Customer Culture	Encourages others to understand customer needs	2	2	1	2	1	1	1	1.4
Customer Culture	Works well with people in your (client's) organization	4	3	4	4	4	3	2	3.4
Customer Culture	Is Service minded	5	4	3	3	3	2	3	3.3
Customer Culture	Is Cooperative	3	3	3	4	3	3	4	3.3

You should by now have a pretty good understanding of the behaviours the business is looking for from your department. You can use these results to help with your recruiting to get the best match of personality.

Recruiting Made Easier

Organisations have their own methods of recruiting but all of them are trying to assess the candidates:

- Relevant Experience
- Technical Ability
- Behaviour Fit
- Personality Profile

Behaviour Fit and Relevant Experience

Your Behaviour Ratings are now worth their weight in gold (well, perhaps silver) especially in helping to assess a candidate's relevant experience and behaviour fit. You can modify your behaviour rating survey to produce direct questions to the candidate. For example:

- Give me an example of where you were service minded
- What steps have you taken to develop yourself?
- How important are ethics in the business environment?
- Give an example of when an important deadline was met.
- How would you encourage teamwork?

Your questions should permit the candidate to provide answers about their mind set and beliefs but also how these have been put into practice in their previous roles. Each answer can be given a score and candidates compared to the behaviour ratings you got from your stakeholders. You won't necessarily have a perfect fit, but you are more likely to have a close fit by using this technique.

Technical Ability

Everyone has a tendency to exaggerate their achievements somewhat. I, for example, would say I am 6 foot, when I'm actually five foot eleven and a half inches. That half inch is important! Slight embellishment is ok, but there has been a tendency over the last few years for people to blatantly lie about their abilities – probably something to do with the rise of online recruiting and related "networking" websites. There have been lots of cases of individuals stating they have a certain technical certification or qualification, which has subsequently been found to be false.

There was a spate a few years ago of people taking exams in other people's names – this happened quite a lot for IT jobs. Definitely worth doing a technical test then but don't make it so hard that only Mensa members can pass. Remember, technical ability can be quickly taught, whereas remoulding someone's core personality is almost impossible. I once went for an IT Manager's job, where the technical test was ludicrously hard. The test was the first stage of the interview. I failed it miserably and hence the interview. Remember, at this stage I hadn't been given the opportunity to talk about my management experience; successful projects and other achievements. I talked briefly with the Finance Director and it turned out that all candidates had failed the test also. It also transpired that their current IT Manager had been with the business for a long time and was moving aside. He wrote the technical test and so it became apparent to me that was showing off to the business and that all candidates were worthless by comparison. Maybe he was angling for a pay rise, I don't know. In effect though, the business was wasting time and money - good candidates were being turned away before they even got chance to speak. Not a case of "Choosing the Right Team".

Personality Profiling

There are various well-known profiling techniques available, such as Thomson International or MBTI. Profiling has it's uses but I don't think it is a good idea to accept or reject a candidate based purely on their profile result. I have seen this in managers and I believe they have missed out on some good candidates. One senior manager rejected a candidate because the profile result suggested the person "wouldn't react well under pressure", but the candidate had been in some high-pressure jobs in the past without being sacked, so he must have been performing ok. Profiling should be taken with a very large pinch of salt (more like a shovel full actually). Personally, I have never used profiling in the interview process because the results can skew your opinion of someone too much.

Now, as they used to say on the UK Crimewatch program, "Don't have Nightmares" but it has been shown that master criminals, con men and psychopaths are very intelligent people and are extremely adept at manipulating others and personality profiling. Relax, I'm not scaremongering here, I'm just making the point that intelligent people can engineer their profile answers to get the result they want. Indeed, with a bit of practise, even a semi-intellectual like me can bend (but not as well as Beckham) the answers.

Profiling should be used as a supplement to the interview process. Certainly do not use it as the initial filter to decide on who should be called in for an interview.

Other Factors to Look Out For

There are a number of smaller factors to look for that shouldn't take long:

- CV Quality. Is it well laid and are there any speeling mistekes?

- Hobbies. Generally, not something that would figure highly on the suitability of a candidate but there are exceptions. If you run a sanctuary for wild deer and the persons hobby is hunting, then they are not in scope (and thankfully nor will your deer be). If you are employing an extreme sports tutor and their great passion is freeform crocheting, you may find they are needled by all the flowing adrenalin.

- Job Stability. How often do they change jobs? It is certainly the case that it is more acceptable for people to swap jobs regularly these days but I am still surprised at how some individuals manage to change jobs every 2-3 years. Recruiting someone and getting them fully up to speed in their role is time consuming and expensive, so I am astounded that organisations take on these "job hoppers". For myself, I want to see some stability in a person's career, but everyone is different.

- Finally, some loose ends to check. Driving License? Appearance? Sociability?

All of these factors can be given a rating.

STEP 1 - CHOOSE THE RIGHT TEAM

Bring it all together

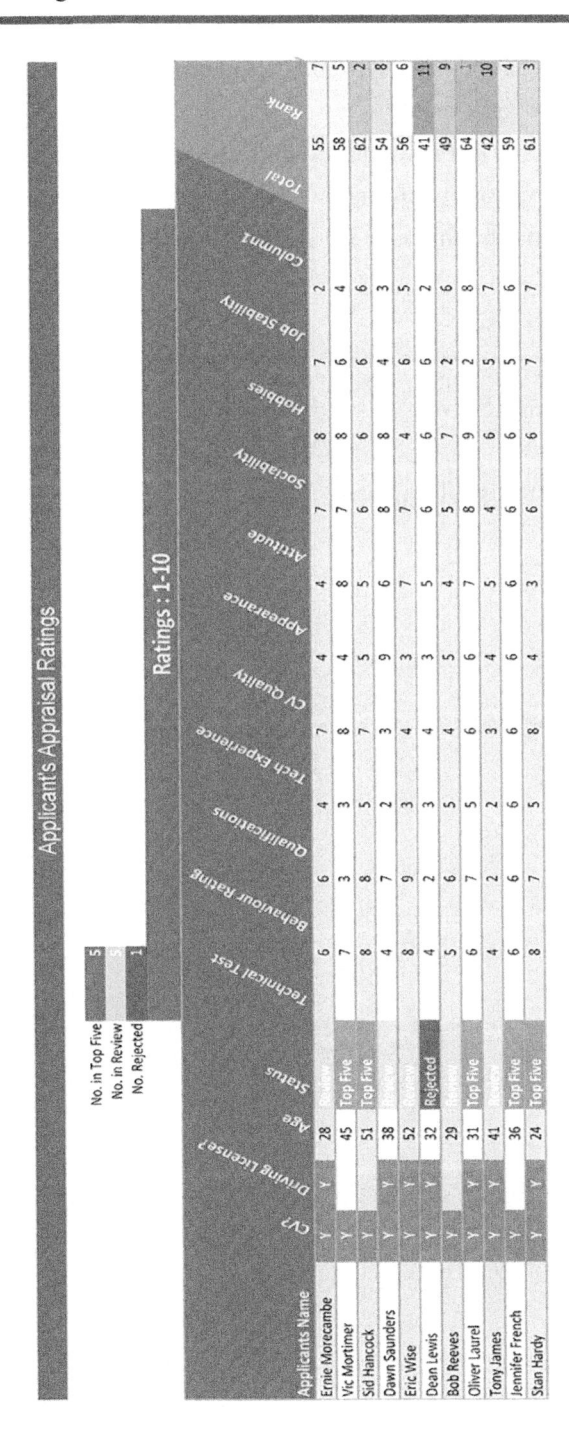

Applicants Name	CV?	Driving License?	Age	Status	Technical Test	Behaviour Rating	Qualifications	Tech Experience	CV Quality	Appearance	Attitude	Sociability	Hobbies	Job Stability	Column1	Total	Rank
Ernie Morecambe	Y	Y	28	Review	6	6	4	7	4	4	7	8	7	2		55	7
Vic Mortimer	Y	Y	45	Top Five	7	3	3	8	4	8	7	8	6	4		58	5
Sid Hancock	Y	Y	51	Top Five	8	8	5	7	5	5	6	6	6	6		62	2
Dawn Saunders	Y	Y	38	Review	4	7	2	3	9	6	8	8	4	3		54	8
Eric Wise	Y	Y	52	Review	8	9	3	4	3	7	7	4	6	5		56	6
Dean Lewis	Y	Y	32	Rejected	4	2	3	4	5	5	6	6	6	2		41	11
Bob Reeves	Y	Y	29	Review	5	6	5	4	5	4	5	7	2	6		49	9
Oliver Laurel	Y	Y	31	Top Five	6	7	2	6	6	7	8	9	2	8		64	1
Tony James	Y	Y	41	Review	4	2	2	3	4	5	4	6	5	7		42	10
Jennifer French	Y	Y	36	Top Five	6	6	6	6	6	6	6	6	5	6		59	4
Stan Hardy	Y	Y	24	Top Five	8	7	5	8	4	3	6	6	7	7		61	3

Applicant's Appraisal Ratings
Ratings : 1-10

No. in Top Five 5
No. in Review   5
No. Rejected   1

All of your previous ratings can be fed into the power of Excel to provide an Applicants Appraisal Dashboard.

This is not a fool proof system but will dramatically help in ensuring you choose the right team.

A blue box has just materialised in the room and some bloke in a long scarf has stepped out claiming to have perfected a fourth dimensional stitch. Who does he think he is? Yes, he does Yoda.

Templates To Use

Behaviour Rating Survey

Applicants Appraisal Template

STEP 2 - DEFINE RESPONSIBILITIES

Your department has a product or service to deliver. There will be a number of sub-tasks to be completed in order to achieve your output. Do you know who is doing what?

It would be unreasonable to expect employees to be accountable for their work, if their responsibilities haven't been clearly defined.

I have been quite shocked at the number of managers I have met over the years who go through the complex and expensive process of trying to recruit the right person for the job only then to ignore them largely in terms of the work they need to do. With these "mis-managers", the employee discovers their tasks by word of mouth from their colleagues or by picking up the work that the rest of the team don't do. In other words, they find their own work niche. Not surprisingly, a team developed like this will be unproductive and not necessarily all pulling in the same direction. Additionally, these bad managers, will look to apportion blame if the departments fails to deliver something, which is hardly fair because people weren't perfectly clear about what they were meant to do!

Defining and subsequently publishing distinct responsibilities is a minor duty but generates a long-lasting profit for the department

Well defined responsibilities will yield:

- Improved efficiency. People know what they have to do, so should appear every morning and just get on with it.

- Assist in balancing workloads.

- Improves knowledge sharing and a transfer of skills. Each sub-task can be given a primary and secondary responsible person. The primary person should be the more experienced and can help to share knowledge with the secondary. Knowledge sharing is extremely important for the long-term stability of a department's output – you don't want to be in a situation where one person owns all the significant knowledge.

- Delineates accountability. If your staff have well defined responsibilities, then there are no excuses for non-delivery.

- Reduced unnecessary competition. It is human nature to focus on doing easier jobs and avoiding the more complex, stress generating work. Your employees will make a bee line for the easier tasks first. Defining responsibilities helps to reduce the race to the bottom and also promotes an equal share of the types of work.

- Better Team Dynamic. Members are less likely to hold misperceptions of others and their workloads. Moreover, people can assist each other when there is a capacity problem.

Firstly, define all the sub-tasks that your team have to perform in order to deliver your department's output. You can then set out your initial draft on who should be the primary and secondary responsible people for these tasks and a pertinent workload for each.

You should end up with a table like this:

STEP 2 - DEFINE RESPONSIBILITIES 41

Responsibilities

Task	Primary	Workload	Secondary	Workload
Review blanket patterns	Mr Hancock	3	Bonny	1
Pick the yarns for patterns	Jerry	2	Mr Wise	2
Distribute yarns for patterns	Mr James	2	Ronnie C	2
Stitch basic squares	Dean	5	Bonny	3
Connect squares according to pattern	Mack	4	Mable	4
Quality check	Ronnie B	1	Bonny	1
Clean finished blanket	Jerry	2	Ronnie C	2
Pack blankets	Mr Hancock	2	Ronnie B	1
Send finished goods off to goods out	Mr Wise	2	Mable	1
		23		**17**

Person Summary

Name	Workload
Bonny	5
Jerry	4
Mable	5
Mack	4
Dean	5
Mr Hancock	5
Mr James	2
Ronnie B	2
Mr Wise	4
Ronnie C	4
An Other	0
An Other	0
	40

You can now discuss this with the team. Some tasks may need to be reallocated. Be ready for your team members to try and re-negotiate their workloads a bit higher (everyone wants to be seen to be busy) – be firm but fair.

When everyone is agreed, then finalise it and publish. It is wise to display it openly (stick it on a noticeboard) as this helps everyone (including clients) to understand who does what.

Revisit the table if there is a change of personnel or the outputs of your department.

Template To Use

Responsibilities

STEP 3 - JOB DESCRIPTIONS

According to most job adverts, you need to have an MBA, 10 years experience, be under 40, have solved the countries deficit issue, be an expert communicator and leader of people, have managed multimillion pound budgets, be born in a leap year and authored two books on saving the whale all to become a junior administrator. Companies (or their assigned recruitment agents) build these ridiculous job descriptions and then (some) fail to have a proper job description in-house to define what the person does. I have experienced this situation and I'm sure many others have too.

I suppose the real skill these days is to see through the fog of jargon and (there's no other word for it) bullshit to get to the actual job on offer. I can imagine the recruitment agents build these opus descriptions to show they are professional and as a means to show why they are worth their large finder's fee.

I could go on about recruitment agents and their sector all day long, so I'll stop before you think I have a chip on my shoulder (mm…too late).

What are the benefits of full and proper job descriptions?

Drawbacks and Benefits

1. How do your staff know what to do? This might seem like a dumb question, but I have seen companies recruit staff and then let them just "find their own way". This opens the door to a number of scenarios:

    a. They get all the work that nobody else wants to do, which tends to be the work that is the most difficult or stressful.

    b. They do work that doesn't add value to your department

c. They do all the menial tasks that provide no personal development at all.

   d. They try to take work that is somebody else's

   e. They do nothing!!! Expensive.

These possibilities lead to inefficient output, heightened tensions and confusion.

1. A proper job description draws the lines in the sand, so everyone knows where their remit lies and people don't cross these lines and get involved in other people's tasks.

2. The described responsibilities can be the basis for the definition of KPIs to be used in the appraisal process.

3. The output efficiency of your department is increased because everyone knows what to deliver.

4. By defining the tasks in the job description then you have, by inference, described the accountability for your team.

5. Assists in appraisals because you have it in writing what someone should be doing, so there is no possibility of a team member saying they didn't know what to do.

6. Helps with recruiting because you can filter out people that don't fit the description.

The Job Description Description

Devoting some time to good job descriptions is a "one-off effort", thereafter the job description can be slightly changed as the role changes.

The description should include:

The Reporting Lines

Who does the person report to and who should report to them? You may be recruiting someone to be a manager of people, so it is important to describe the team that reports to them.

As an interesting aside here, I know of some larger companies that get this so wrong that you could almost call it anarchy. One friend of mine had 2 bosses. One was functional – ie they determined what work my friend should do and the expected results from it. The other was for doing all the managerial stuff, like 1:1s , appraisals etc. For the 1:1 and appraisals to have any use, then the first boss had to report to the 2nd boss about how well my friend had performed and delivered. Not surprisingly, these two bosses didn't always get round to this in time for the 1:1 or appraisal, so my friend was left feeling detached and confused – indeed they didn't feel like they had a boss at all!! An employee should have a clear line of sight to their 1 boss.

Authority Levels

Do they have a budget?

What computer permissions should they have?

What is their spend limit without needing further authorisation?

Main interactions

List the departments, groups and key individuals that the person will interact with in the delivery of their tasks.

Behaviours

What are the expected behaviours? Don't confuse these with technical skill – they will be defined later. These behaviours will depend on the type of department you manage but should have been defined before the recruitment process began by asking your stakeholders to define the behaviours they want from your department. Here are some sample behaviours:

- Excellent communication skills.
- Is Service minded.
- Is Cooperative.
- Believes in self-development.
- Demonstrates honesty.
- Is Trustworthy.
- Has a Positive mindset.
- Correctly prioritises work.
- Is Organised.
- Reacts swiftly to changing business needs.
- Is Consistent

Technical skills

These will be very much determined by whatever your department does. You should list the technical requirements including any professional qualifications

Responsibilities

Here you list all the tasks or work that the person has to deliver. This section will probably take the longest to complete as you have break down your final outputs into the pertinent sub-tasks.

After devoting so much effort in defining good quality job descriptions, then don't simply file them away. Show them to your team and make sure that everyone knows (and has a copy of) their job description. You will only receive the benefits described above if your employees have received their relevant description.

You may have to revisit the descriptions every now and then to ensure they fit with the business. Inclusion is always good, so get your team involved in the redefinition of descriptions.

Template To Use

Job Description Template

STEP 4 - ARE YOUR 1:1S REALLY JUST 0:1S?

You walk into your 1:1 with your boss, sit down and he says "Right, what do you want to talk about?". My gut instinct is to reply "What a useless boss you are. I've seen better people skills from Basil Fawlty having a bad day". I don't say it of course – I bite my tongue, take some Valium, have a massage then remember my professionalism and give a calm reply, which, seriously, should be "What do YOU want to talk about?"

I've had 1:1s with my boss just like this and I know from colleagues that it is happening in all companies of all sizes every day. I have attended a few leadership courses and have been amazed that senior managers hold these "open nature" 1:1s and utterly incredulous that some don't do 1:1s at all and have never even thought about it. As an extreme example, I once met a Director who had numerous staff about 60 miles from where she was based. She had been in the job for a year and couldn't get them to gel as a department. I asked her how often she met them – her answer made my head explode – "I've never been"!! When I suggested that she should perhaps, maybe, if the sun is shining go and introduce herself, her response was "Out of the Question"! I washed my hands of her issue there and then (after I had stopped staring with my mouth open). Some people are beyond help.

A 1:1 is the only opportunity for your staff member to have quality time with their leader. The above anecdote conveys a manager who is unprepared; is not committed to the development of his staff; doesn't value the 1:1 and hence doesn't value his staff members. The employee will leave the 0:1 feeling completely devalued and unmotivated. This will directly affect individual and team performance.

"Open Nature" 1:1s will result in chatting about Coronation Street or Wayne Rooney's latest goal, which is all very nice, but can be done round the water cooler. Unfortunately, the conversation will also stray to the dark side – moaning about the performance of individuals and/or departments; rumours and negative gossip. This is probably a sign that the staff member is frustrated with the 0:1 and it's the manager's job to uphold a positive culture.

Regular, structured 1:1s are one of the foundations of a productive and happy team.

Here is the structure I have used which proved to be very effective. You can of course cherry pick and/or completely disagree – we can discuss our differences in a 1:1 maybe?

KPI Performance. How have they performed against their individual and department KPIs?

Milestone or Project Progress. Aside from their normal activities do they do other work? Is it SMART based? Ask for a progress report. You may have to prod them a bit to stay on track.

Development. How are they fairing against the development plan you set at their yearly appraisal? More prodding maybe required.

Issues. Are they struggling with something technical or a relationship with a colleague? Are there some barriers to hinder their progress?

Yearly Appraisal Score. Assuming your company provides an annual appraisal with some kind of rating – a big tip I learned from a very good manager – there should be no surprises for the employee at the appraisal. The person thinks they are working well all year only to be told they are under performing at the end of the year. This is completely unfair and demoralising to the point that their productivity will be reduced for the forthcoming year. Thoughts of "What's the point in me trying" clouding their spirit every day. So, give them an unofficial rating each month to convey how they are performing.

Feedback. A verbal statement and praise (if due) from you about how they are doing.

Reverse Feedback. Their opportunity to tell you how you are doing. I can hear the alarm bells chiming and you are right, this is potentially a dangerous practice. Clearly, they cannot comment on your dress sense or the fact that you eat with your mouth open (small hint – close your mouth) – they can only comment on your abilities as a manager and leader. To ensure they stay professional you should write some guidelines about what they can comment on – see the template "Reverse Feedback Topic List". Personal experience has shown me that it takes a while for employees to get used to the idea of criticising their boss until they can trust you enough to know that you won't use their opinions against them in the future (and of course you mustn't). It's daring to ask for suggestions to improve your performance, but how else will you know if you are managing properly?

News From Above. Company news you can waterfall down

AOB. Now is the time for Wayne Rooney chat if the employee has nothing else to bring up. I'm not limiting it to Wayne Rooney you understand – in fact I don't think I have every talked about him – until now it seems.

I had 1:1s with my staff every month for 1 hour and have found that you can fit all of the above in quite easily.

Record It

All this should be recorded somewhere for future reference. You can use the provided 1:1 template to your employee – it is their responsibility to fill it in, not yours. Ensure they save it somewhere away from the eyes of their colleagues – 1:1 information is private.

Templates

1:1 Template

Reverse Feedback Topic List

I'm off to put on my Number 10 shirt...damn I'm infected!

STEP 5 - YEARLY APPRAISALS

Surprise Surprise!!!!!

Nope. All wrong. The opposite. One of the key aspects of the yearly appraisal is that there should be no surprises at all. Indeed, surprise is the wrong word – more like bombshell.

Throughout the year, the employee believes they are delivering to standard and you are happy with their performance. Then, in the yearly appraisal, you rate them as below par with some additional criticisms. This is the bombshell and it will leave a very big crater in your employee's motivation going forward. Immediately on hearing the news, you employee will feel shocked; disbelief; anger (rightly so); demotivated and belittled.

Any manager that delivers nasty surprises in the yearly appraisal has a long way to go to improve their performance and is THE most damaging tactic on individual and team spirit. It is completely unfair and demoralising to the point that their productivity will be reduced for the forthcoming year. Thoughts of "What's the point in me trying" clouding their motivation every day. It also evaporates any trust and respect that employees have for the manager.

I have experienced this myself and have heard of other managers doing it. I have met some managers who give low ratings in the appraisal so they can justify who gets a performance related bonus. Generally speaking, a manager will be given a pot of money for the bonus and it is their decision who gets a slice. By handing out low appraisal ratings, they can ensure their "favoured" team members get a bigger slice. The worst example I saw of this was a manager who had some team members in his home country and some members in another country. He gave all the people in the foreign country a low rating to ensure he could split the bonus amongst the "home grown" staff.

So, to empty the glass that is already half empty – dropping bombshells in the yearly appraisal is one of the worst managerial behaviours there is. It shows a lack of engagement and commitment to the team and will undo every other positive managerial behaviour you try to implement. I'm an optimist, so now we'll think of it from the glass half full perspective. The simplest solution to all of the above is to simply not drop any bombs.

The Correct Way

The yearly appraisal usually has 2 elements – to review and appraise performance for the year just gone and then to look forward to the coming year.

The looking back element, "the appraisal", should be painless and quick if you act like a boy scout. Be Prepared!

Prepare by:

- Giving the employee an unofficial appraisal rating in all their 1:1s throughout the year. This shows them where they are heading. They may want to aim for a higher appraisal rating at the end of the year, so you can discuss what they need to achieve in order to get there.

- Review the development progress of the person over the year.

- Review the KPI performance over the year.

- Review their milestone achievements over the year. You may have to ask your staff member to see their logbook to get the milestones.

- Check any 360° reviews for the person.

Most of these duties can be completed in the run up to the appraisal – the only yearly commitment is the unofficial rating in the regular 1:1s.

The Appraisal Content

Whether electronic or paper based, your appraisal system should cover:

Looking Back

Individual KPIs for the year. Your department will have some KPIS set for delivery of your product or service. Generally, these department KPIs can be set as individual ones. There may be completely personal ones depending on the person's role.

Responsibilities. It is easy to list these from the job description. What are the tasks that the person does throughout the year?

Development Progress. Everyone should have some form of development. How is the progress?

Additional Comments or Notes. List the Milestone Achievements or any other form of worded criticism or praise that cannot be expressed as a simple numeric rating.

Overall Appraisal Score. Your organisation will have a scoring scheme. 1-5 or 1-10 or even A-E. There may even be a description of what is required to attain each score. I once gave an employee of mine a rating that meant he was "on par" – ie he had performed to an acceptable standard. He was a little disgruntled because he believed he deserved a rating of "above par". I sent him the descriptions of ratings that showed what behaviours needed to be displayed in order to achieve each rating. After he read it, he agreed with the score I had given him.

Looking Forward

Career Aspiration. What does the person want to be doing in the 3-5 years? Is it realistic? Can they really be CEO within 3 years?

Development Plan. What development to achieve over the coming year? Is it realistic?

Support From Manager. How can you offer support to the person to contribute towards their career aspiration and development plan? This could be in the form of an addition to the budget or an allowance of extra time.

Individual KPIs for the year. What are the measurable KPIs for the forthcoming year?

Responsibilities. Unless a role has changed markedly, then the list of responsibilities should remain quite static – so the same as the year just gone.

The Appraisal Session

It is important for your team to understand the importance of their yearly appraisal, so it is your job to emphasise this leading up to the session. They need to put some time in preparing all their self-ratings for the year looking back but more importantly to decide on their career aspirations and development requirements. It is worth stressing that development wishes should be in line with their job role. If they are a master crocheter then they shouldn't be asking to take an HGV license.

Leading up to the appraisal, you should decide on all the ratings for each section. Your employee should do the same. During the session, you may have some differences in the two ratings (but the differences should be small) which can be discussed and agreed upon. No surprises though, remember?

If you have been diligent throughout the year, then the looking back section should be painless and straight forward. Potentially, a stumbling block could arise if the person has an unrealistic impression of how they are doing. The evidence from KPI performance, milestone achievements and 360° review results should help with these discussions as they are documented evidence of performance and behaviours.

The "Looking Forward" section will take more time as career aspirations and development requirements will require some discussion and compromise agreements. Be prepared to make some compromises yourself – if your employee is the one making all the concessions then you will appear to be non-cooperative and narrow minded.

After The Session

After the meeting, you should ensure that you deliver your side of the bargain, which could include:

- Officially documenting the appraisal ratings, comments etc. Employees will be aggravated if they can't see their appraisal has been documented weeks after the session took place.

- Allocating some money in the budget for development.

- Providing some extra time to ensure development progresses.

- Updating your development plans.

- Delivering anything else you have agreed in the session.

- Setting a date for a mid-year appraisal session. The mid-year briefly touches on the "looking back" element in respect of whether the person is working acceptably. No official rating is given – this only happens at the full appraisal. More focus will be on the "looking forward" element to ensure everything is on track with the plans set from the last appraisal = ie development.

Appraisals have the greatest impact on team dynamic and individual performance so be engaged all year; do your homework; remain impartial and be fair and you won't have any worries.

And on that bombshell... what could possibly go wrong? (Where have I heard that before?)

Template To Use

Yearly Appraisal Template

STEP 6 - DEPARTMENT MEETING

Over the years I have met a number of managers and directors who are so far out of touch with their staff and what it means to be a manager of people that I have really thought they shouldn't be in management at all. I once met a director who had a team of 19 people spread over 2 sites approximately 60 miles apart who had never had a department meeting. I have also met numerous other managers who haven't held them too. How can a manger expect a group of people to all work together in the same direction if they never come together to discuss things? It's incredible how many managers have no understanding of the basics.

The department meeting is one of the basic deliverables of a manager. It will gel your people together into a collaborative workforce.

How Often and How Long?

Getting all your staff together daily or weekly for a quick roundup is acceptable, especially if your department function requires it. It would suggest, however, that these meetings should be lean and mean – a quick review of the day's tasks, a short review of yesterday's performance etc.

A full department meeting is an opportunity to review KPI performance, appraise goal/project work status, inform the department of news about the organisation, brainstorm, focus on certain topics etc. Done properly, this is too much to fit into a daily or weekly meeting. I held my department meetings monthly because there is enough time between each meeting for progress to be made and is not too disruptive to normal daily operations. If you manage disparate groups who are separated by distance and time zones, then a monthly meeting may be problematic. As a minimum, you should hold a full department meeting once a quarter.

Groups of people tend to have a pessimistic view of other groups (even in the same department) especially if they are separated by time, language and culture. If these perceptions are allowed to mature, then you can end up with groups working in silos and the collaboration is reduced.

It's important then to break down these misconceptions by removing the barriers of geography, time, culture and language. If you have remote teams, use technology to improve attendance. Video conferencing is widespread these days, so invite everyone in your team, regardless of their time zone. Sometimes this is difficult if you have teams spread all round the world – finding a time to suite all is difficult. Expecting employees in the Americas to join a meeting at 10pm, while your employees in the Far East have to join at 4am is asking a lot. To assist with this problem, you could nominate one person from each remote region to attend and then it is their responsibility to waterfall the meeting outputs to their colleagues in the same time zone. You can rota this role, so the same person doesn't have to stay up till 2am every month. (Energy drinks at the ready).

I will list below some suggestions as to the structure of the meeting. With this structure in mind, our department meetings were scheduled for 3 hours, once per month.

Budget permitting, it is immensely valuable to get your team in to the same room at least twice a year. I realise that this can be expensive if your staff are all over the world, so this will greatly depend on your organisation's finances but if you have members globally, then this suggests you work for a multi-national, so the money should be there. Always put some money in your budget for these international meetings because the pay-offs in terms of productivity, collaboration, team dynamic and communication far out way the actual outlay. You can set aside a whole day for this meeting to cover all the normal topics plus additional ones such as brainstorming sessions, how to improve your services, development plans for the coming year, improving your collaboration or do some joint training, like time management. If the budget will run to it, socialise in the evening and stay overnight. Great benefits are to be reaped from this social "gluing".

Delegation and Development

Every meeting needs a Chairperson and a note taker. A free way (always the best way) to offer staff development is to hand the reigns over to them to organise the meetings. Setup a rota so that each staff member has the opportunity to chair the meeting and be the note taker (you should include yourself in the rota, so the staff can see how you run the meeting). You can then just be an attendee of the meeting which affords you the opportunity to watch staff members and (quietly) appraise their organisational abilities. There is an art to delegation – there is a fine line between good delegation and just offloading onto your staff. Initially, there may be some reservations from certain employees about having to take on these tasks, but my experience is that they generally get to enjoy the added responsibility and power (just hope the power doesn't go to their heads).

To ensure the meeting is as fruitful as possible, you will have to define the roles of the Chairperson and Note taker:

Chairperson. Has to ensure all invites are sent out and that people have responded. Book all the meeting rooms and video conference units. Gather information from all members to develop the agenda. Ensure all documentation is distributed before the meeting. Run the meeting according to the schedule and times. Manage the communication in the meeting - you don't want people talking over each other or becoming unprofessional. This will also include the responsibility to minimise on chatter – some socialising is good, but the outcomes of the meeting will be reduced if members spend all their time talking about the latest reality TV show.

Note Taker. Your standpoint may be that you want everything that is said to be minuted. My preference is to only minute important comments or actions. Make sure your note taker understands the level of minuting that you want. It is very important that the outputs from the meeting (especially the actions) are written down and distributed. It is the Note Takers job to do this.

The Structure

The essence of the meeting is to review what we have done, assess where we are going, inform and build collaboration. As said previously, my monthly meetings lasted 3 hours, with this structure:

KPI or Performance Review. This is a review of the department only – DO NOT review individual's performance in front of everyone else. Your department will have expected outcomes, so it is imperative you review how you are doing. This section should take no longer than 15 minutes.

Task Updates and Workload Check. Aside from the daily routine work, it is likely your staff will have additional tasks (which are really small projects). My team had an average of 20 tasks all running concurrently. Every attendee provides a highlighted review of their task progress – it's important to stress that you don't need to hear the minutiae of the work as this could take days to get through. They should bring up any hindrances to their tasks, thereby giving the rest of the team the chance to offer solutions. You will be amazed at how inventive people can be and most enjoy the opportunity of being supportive. Your Chairperson will need to monitor the time closely here because discussions can develop with a possibility of the schedule slipping.

When these tasks are originally handed out (or hopefully, people will volunteer for them), they will have various workloads placed on them. Some tasks will be larger than others and will take more time. Thus, each task should have a workload weighting (which may have to be reviewed as the task progresses). The tasks for each person are recorded and thus their workload can be calculated. During the meeting, perform a sanity check of current workloads to ensure all staff are equally busy. Approx. timing 40 minutes.

News from Above. The department needs to know what is happening in the rest of the business, particularly strategy news about where your organisation is going. Approx. timing 15 minutes.

Goals/Project Status Review. Some staff will be involved in official projects. The objective here is the same as the task updates – a highlighted review of progress and potential obstacles. Generally, there won't be much discussion about the big projects or goals because they will be outside the circle of influence of your other staff members. Approx. timing 40 minutes

Spotlight Topics. This is an open slot in the meeting that you may not utilise in each meeting. This is an opportunity to focus in on one or two large topics that need discussion. It could be connected with organisational changes, major projects, updated strategies or new IT systems. Approx. Timing 40 minutes.

Miscellaneous/AOB. I won't insult your intelligence by describing what this is. Approx. Timing 15 minutes

Review the Format

Over a period of time it may become obvious that certain elements of the meeting don't work. Don't be afraid to review the success of the meeting or to change elements. Ask your staff for their viewpoints as they will possibly have different perceptions than yourself.

Department meetings should yield a mutual sense of collaboration, productivity, direction and fun. And the staff get to do all the work (well, mostly) ......ahhh, delegation!! J

Template To Use

Department Meeting Template

STEP 7 - DELEGATION

There are two obvious signs that you have got your delegation all wrong:

1. You are working long hours, feel stressed and your department repeatedly fails on deadlines or KPIs while your staff stick to their 9-5. You are probably a micro-manager, are unable to let go of work which will result in numerous other issues with your team. If you look up delegation on the internet, this scenario is often mentioned as the key sign that you are not able to delegate properly. This is one extreme example of poor delegation.

2. Signs of the other extreme are that you only work 9-5; there are scuff marks on your desk where you regularly put your feet up; you are the main source of funny videos on Youtube and you are spending a lot of time recruiting people because your staff turnover is high. There is a fair chance here that you are unfairly overloading ALL the work to your team to make your workload as small as possible.

Someone once said that delegation is an art, and this is true but there are techniques for us unartistic types to monitor how we are doing. In simpler terms, the "art" is getting the balance right and there are tools to help you get there.

What is Delegation?

Can you deliver everything your department needs to produce, by yourself, in normal office hours? You can? Then you don't need a team, so you can ignore this chapter and buy a book about firing people.

I have to assume that your answer was no and that you have a team. Delegation then is distributing work while ensuring that everyone has a fair workload balance and results in:

- Everyone (including you) having a fair and evenly distributed workload

- Providing development opportunities to your team

- Your department delivers on time and within budget

- Your cache with your team is high because they can see you believe in their abilities

- Helping you to retain your team.

What Can You Delegate?

Surely these are all the boring, menial tasks that you find uninteresting or too difficult leaving you with interesting, challenging work that you enjoy? Noooo. It is true that you will have to release work that you enjoy, so if you are a Pivot table fanatic but Ronnie is better at data analysis, then you will have to let go of your Excel crush.

What to delegate:

- Work that you shouldn't be doing as a manager. Your department has something to deliver and it is your job to ensure it gets produced on time and within budget. It doesn't mean that you do all the work to deliver it. Your job is to ensure that your team does. Sometimes this means that you will give people menial or repetitive tasks, and that's ok, so long as you delegate the challenging and interesting work too.

- Any task that provides a development opportunity for your staff, no matter how small the development

- Anything where one of your team has better skills than you

- Work that is challenging and interesting. Ensure that your chosen person has the right skills otherwise they will fail (and so will you). I have seen managers delegate work for no other reason that they are daunted by the task and don't want to face the challenge.

Sometimes there will be an opportunity to delegate but the output is extremely important to your department and you may feel you are the best suited to the job. In this case, do the work jointly with a team member. I once had to negotiate a new large mobile phone contract with some sizeable sums of money involved. On the first anniversary, I did the work in conjunction with one of my team members. Second time around, because I was safe in the knowledge that he knew the process, he took the lead with another team member, so the knowledge was being shared.

How to Delegate

Before you delegate something, ask yourself a few questions:

- Are you unfairly offloading? Delegation is not about pushing all the work away for others to complete so be careful that you don't fall into this trap. The difference between good delegation and unfairly dumping on people is a fine one.

- Who has the best skillset for the task in hand? If you have to produce 50 crocheted blankets with a bumpy textured granule stitch, then don't give the job to someone who thinks that crocheting is to do with hitting a ball through a hoop with a hammer. Obvious.

- Is this task repetitive, boring or menial? If it is, make sure your people all have a fair share.

- Who has the right mind set for the job? We all think we have enough work, so most people will not buy you chocolates for stuffing their in-tray. What you are looking for is for the people who will accept the work and do the best they can. Anyone that is going to continuously grumble about it will in all likeliness not deliver, so choose wisely.

- Will you be able to properly let go of the task? If not, why not? If the task or project is vital to the department's output, then consider co-working with one of your team on it.

- How will you measure the success of the task? What are the goals or KPIs that can measure the success? You should definitely discuss this with the chosen staff member(s), but as with all managerial duties, it is best if you can prepare some in advance.

Delegating Channels

There are a number of ways to delegate, each has it's merits and pitfalls:

- By email. Very easy to do – so easy in fact that you could fall into the trap of just clearing your inbox and expecting everyone else to do everything. This is the most widely used channel of delegating and there is nothing wrong with it per se – just use it with caution. I have seen so many bosses write "Please deal with this" which is an offhanded way to give someone more work to do.

- In a 1:1. Much more personal than email and provides an opportunity to discuss workloads, potential hurdles and ways to measure success.

- Team Meetings and brainstorming sessions. Interesting arenas these because your staff get the opportunity to volunteer for work rather then you dividing it up. Delegation by proxy - brilliant!

Be Specific

As with any task or project, specifics need to be defined. Just because you understand what is required doesn't mean that your chosen person does, so clear communication is very important.

Ensure you define (in collusion with your chosen person):

- The deadline

- The expected outputs or deliverables

- A reporting or feedback schedule

- Who to communicate with during the period to gain all the inputs required

- Any possible hurdles and potential remedies to them

Who to Delegate to

Some of the selection criteria has already been mentioned, but to clarify, when selecting a person, you should assess:

- Their workload – do they have the spare capacity for the work? A workload spreadsheet to monitor all workloads should help here.

- Their skillset is right for the task

- They will have a willing mindset

- The development opportunity fits their desired development path

Follow Up

This could be the most important element of delegation because it will provide a lot of answers to questions such as:

- How is the task progressing? Will it be delivered on time and in budget?

- Is the person sinking or staying afloat?

- What root causes are preventing a good result? Are they personal or technical in nature?

- Can the task be refined to produce a better outcome?

- Would joint work help the task and/or person towards a better result?

- What lessons can be learnt about this delegation? Was there a good fit between person and task?

You can follow up during 1:1s, team meetings or project reviews.

How to Measure if Delegation is Working

There is no absolute KPI to measure your delegation skills but there a number of other factors that can be quantified that result in a way of grading your delegation.

Employee Survey. Any good employee survey should ask staff about their immediate manager's performance including a direct question about their delegating skills. If your organisation's survey does not include this question, then put forward a suggestion to have it included. There is no better method of having a direct grading from your staff. I once got a score of 98% for my delegation skills from my staff, which gave me concerns that someone could interpret this result as me just offloading everything. (I have found from employee surveys that people do interpret questions very differently). I talked to my staff about the high score to ascertain whether they thought I was offloading everything to them – it turns out that they didn't, and the score was a good result. However, I was pleased when the result went down the following year to 91% - the only time I wanted a lower score on a survey!

Reverse Feedback. A reverse feedback element should be included in 1:1s in which staff can give you feedback on your performance. Your delegation skills can be included.

Workload Check. Keeping a record of everyone's (including your own) workload can be recorded in a spreadsheet. There should not be any big variances, especially between yourself and your people. Indeed, it is a good PR exercise to have a workload that is slightly higher than your staff.

Self-Analysis. I'm not suggesting you sit and contemplate your navel (and you certainly wouldn't want to contemplate mine), but a few simple self-assessments should put your mind at rest (or not if you've got it all wrong):

- Do you regularly work long hours?

- Do you staff regularly work long hours?

- How often are you involved in the actual outputs of your department?

- Are the workloads balanced for all?

- Have you got good staff retention?

- Does your department regularly deliver on time and within budget?

- Does your team all pull in the same direction?

- Is the team harmonious?

- Do you intervene in employee's work?

You can bring all of these elements into a spreadsheet to monitor your effectiveness. To gain any real value from it, you need to answer honestly – if you exaggerate your scores, you are only kidding yourself, so be realistic. You should end up with something like this:

STEP 7 - DELEGATION

Your Delegation Rating
50.00% Mediocre Score - Which focus Area is Letting You Down?

		Score Between 1 and 10	Tips
Employee Survey Result	As %	50	Get this from the Employee Survey if you have one. If not, put 0
Average Staff Workload	As %	30	You can pull this from your workload calculator spreadsheet
Your Average Workload	As %	35	You can pull this from your workload calculator spreadsheet
Number of Projects Delivered on Time	As %	40	You can pull this from your projects stats
Staff Retention	As %	41	How many staff still remain out the total number that have been employed?
Team Harmony	As %	49	Estimate. How well do your staff work together and all pulling in the same direction
Your delegation abilities feedback received	As %	45	Estimate this based on the verbal reverse feedback you get from staff in 1:1 sessions
Do you work long hours?	Score between 0 and 5	2	How many of the 5 working days do you regularly work longer hours?
Do you staff reularly work long hours?	Score between 0 and 5	2	How many of the 5 working days do your staff work longer hours?
How ofter do you produce actual outputs of the department?	Score between 0 and 40	15	Assuming a 40 hour week, how many hours do you spend delivering the output of your department?
How often do you intervene in employees work?	Score between 0 and 5	1	Estimate on a scale of 0 and 5. 0=I never intervene, 5=I intervene on a regular basis.

Summary

Delegation is the bedrock of a functioning department. Get it wrong and your department will not deliver on time; have uneven workloads leading to heightened stress levels and will ultimately lead to poor staff retention.

Get it right, however, and the benefits are myriad in nature:

- The department is productive and efficient

- The workload is shared equally

- Stress levels are reduced

- Staff retention improves

- Staff are developed and nurtured

- Your respect and trust grows with your team

- You have empowered employees

The process in summary is:

1. Choose a task to Delegate

2. Decide on who the best person is

3. Communicate the specifics

4. Delegate

5. DON'T INTERFERE

6. Follow up and Appraise

I've got a bad scuff mark on my desk – anyone got any polish?

Template To Use

Delegation Rating

STEP 8 - GOAL SETTING

What is a Goal?

In football, it's £416,000!! Wayne Rooney earns £12.7 million a year and averages 31 goals in the same time. Damn good work if you can get it.

In business, I'm afraid you will get paid less and there is a lot more paperwork.

A goal is NOT something to be associated with the daily routine of work. So, "Process 100 invoices a week" or "Polish 26 crankshafts a week" are not goals – they are KPIs and should be written into job specs. Goals should be set outside of the normal expected deliverables of a job. If handled correctly, setting and achieving goals can be very rewarding for staff members because it gives them tasks that are more rewarding and interesting than their routine work.

To set a goal, you should arrange a meeting (privately in a meeting room) with yourself and the employee(s) who will be involved. Set a time limit for the meeting - usually 1 hour is enough unless it's a particularly large task. The goal defined should be a collaboration between yourself and the staff member. It's important they contribute fully in the meeting because they will then be fully "bought into" the idea.

A goal is a target set that should be specific, relevant and achievable. In this world of Big Data (what does that actually mean?), if you enter 'Goal Setting Techniques" into Google, you will get 10.7 million hits (who cares?). As usual, I will talk through one technique, which is simple and effective.

SMART

"S" Specific. A goal has to be specific. It would be unwise and unfair to set goals without specific parameters. You cannot set goals like "Improve Cash flow" or "Replace all the desks in the office" because they open to interpretation issues. How will your staff member know if they have hit target? What's the budget for the desks? What type and style of desk? Who else will be involved? When should this be accomplished?

Thus, when setting the goal, these questions should be answered:

1. What is to be accomplished?

2. Who is involved? Or Who will it affect?

3. Where will it take place?

4. When should it be accomplished by?

5. How much will it cost?

6. Any other (specific) elements that affect the outcome.

"M" Measurable. How do you know if the goal is successful? The questions you ask in the Specific section should provide some measurable targets to aim for.

From our desk replacement example:

1. Replace 150 desks in HQ with electrically powered raising desks in dull grey. (This company obviously has too much money and no imagination).

2. The staff member is involved alongside the furniture sales rep and the departmental managers

3. HQ – 2nd and 3rd floor

4. 31st February 2016

5. £375,000 (They have way too much money – probably merchant bankers)

6. Define a staged rollout plan with the departments to minimise disruption.

7. etc

"A" Attainable/Achievable. You can't say "Clean all the office windows by this time tomorrow" if you work in The Shard. Be realistic. Goals should push your staff but within reason. You and they should see goal setting as a way for them to develop and/or attain skills that they can utilise in the future (as well as delivering something of value to the department and thus, the company). It's very important then to not set goals that are below the capabilities of the person. This will result in them feeling demeaned and raise questions in their head such as "Why is the boss giving me this shit to do?" You have to ensure that the person will realistically be able to succeed so ensure you both understand any outside influences that could affect the outcome. "Improving Cashflow" will entail involvement from all departments. Will your staff member realistically be able to influence all departmental managers to be involved? What other potential obstacles are there? You should brainstorm all outside influences and potential hindrances and either decide on solutions to these or accept that some hindrances may not be solved and could affect the outcome of the goal. In this case, you may have to redefine the measurables.

"R" Realistic/Relevant. Here is a chance to go over what you have already discussed and review if the goals set are realistic. The outcome will depend on many factors, such as the measurable you have set, outside influences, potential obstacles and the skillset of your staff member. Do all these factors work together? There is no point asking someone to improve the inter-departmental relationships of the department if they are shy and quiet. With all the factors considered, it is quite common at this point, to change the measurables of the goal.

What is the relevancy of this goal to your department and the company? Does this goal work towards or against other goals you have set? If you have already fixed a department vision, then does this goal contribute? Most importantly, does this goal work with or against the company's goals? Don't buy the 150 desks if the company's goal is to improve cashflow!! I once saw a colleague of mine asked to physically clean over 100 computers, and yet they would be retired in a month's time because they were being replaced. Pointless exercise.

"T" Time Bound. You will probably already have discussed this in the measurables section, but a target date is fundamental. The employee needs to be able to plan their time, but the main reason for the deadline is accountability.

More Work For You

As the manager you have additional questions and responsibilities to ensure the goals are successful.

Fair and Consistent Goals? Staff members will compare their own goals to those of their colleagues – you have to ensure that you have defined goals that are objective, equal and fair. If Bonny and Clyde are two equally capable employees and you have asked Bonny to ensure the toilets are cleaned daily, but Clyde gets to organise a new office move, then expect some backlash.

Publish all Goals. Everyone should know all goals in the department. Transparency and knowledge sharing are one of the key factors in a department's success. The additional benefit is that everyone can see how they are doing compared to their colleagues – a bit of healthy competition is good and improves accountability and productivity (something we are continually told we are poor at in the UK). Before you publish however, there are two factors you need to consider:

1. Are the goals fair and consistent?

2. Not all goals will be focused on delivering something of value to the department. Occasionally, usually as a result of a coaching session, some goals will be agreed with an employee that are more personal. There could have been an issue with relationships or a lack of technical knowledge or even problems at home for the employee. Goals can be set to help with these types of situations. Technical training, communication training, or in the case of the person with problems at home, goals that give them the opportunity to work alone (or be surrounded by people). This could get too complicated to explain here, but suffice to say, goals can be set that you definitely SHOULDN'T publish because they could cause embarrassment.

Review and Appraise. Probably the most important task for you as the manager. You cannot set goals and then wash your hands of them – this will portray completely the wrong message to your staff. If you show no interest in the outcome, then the question is, why did you bother to set the goal in the first place? Believe me, your staff will be asking the same question too. Some Brownie points lost there. There are plenty of opportunities to review and appraise - 1:1s, yearly appraisals, department meetings and sometimes you will have to organise a separate review meeting if the goal involves a lot of work. You should definitely set time aside in the regular 1:1s to discuss progress with the goal.

Set Time Aside. All people like to stay in their comfort zone, so your employees will naturally focus on their daily tasks because they know what they are doing. Because goals should push your employees to do something irregular, they can struggle to self-start the work towards the goal. With this in mind, you should give them dedicated time to work on the goal, so block out periods in the week for dedicated goal work time. This is especially important if their role normally entails a lot of disruptions or if your department's function is on the frontline.

An IT Support department will naturally receive lots of new interactions with the business – new service calls, phone calls, emails from IT users, employees walking in with IT issues. This is a difficult environment for your staff to find the time to do goal work unless you set aside the time for them. Set up a simple weekly plan of who is working on what and publish it to the whole department. All your staff members should know that Joe is doing dedicated project/goal work on Tuesday afternoons from 2pm till 4pm. It will be their responsibility to ensure he is not disturbed during that time. Joe can book himself into a meeting room to ensure he gets the dedicated time. Ensuring your staff have time to work on the goals is paramount.

Log It. We all have selective memories and as we get older, we, erm, "What was it?", oy yeah, forget things! Staff log books are a great idea I picked up on a few years ago. I will write more about this later, but one section of the log book is called Milestones. All milestone events in the year should be recorded here. These can be projects completed, certifications passed, high KPI results and of course goal outcomes. If the milestones are recorded faithfully during the year, then the yearly appraisal becomes much easier for both the manager and the staff member because the year's achievements are in one snapshot.

Goals are usually set to achieve something outside of the normal routine. If all your staff do is the routine work, then your department is not improving. You should thus equate successful goal achievement to be fundamental to your department's success. £416,000 a time – I'm off to buy some football boots.

Template To Use

SMART Goals Template

STEP 9 - STAFF DEVELOPMENT

Calling all whittlers – Sorry but this is not about improving your sticks.

Staff development is actually an investment, but with a difference. Unlike the financial type, investing in your people is almost risk free. If you develop your staff, you are almost guaranteed to reap the many benefits from doing so.

There will be rare occasions when you invest some time and money into an individual who then jumps ship almost immediately. This can happen if the person passes a professional certification that has a high value in the job market, so some foresight and common sense is required. If a person needs a specific, highly marketable, certification to carry out their job at your organisation, then you have no option but to take the risk. If their request for this certification does not fit your organisation's roadmap, then you are entitled to refuse this request. If all other aspects of their job experience is positive (i.e. salary, environment, interesting work and of course the most important...a good boss), then the risk still remains low because people don't go looking for other jobs if the grass is quite green already where they currently work.

The Benefits of Staff Development

Your posture improves? (No, this is not about sticks!) You can buy those curved metal badges from fell walking gift shops? (NO, this is NOT about sticks!).

The benefits are varied:

- I was once asked by a Director what proof I had that my staff were proficient enough to deliver the services they were supposed to. Formal certifications then, provide a rubber stamp of your team's validity to deliver the products or services of your department. Certifications are a stamp of quality. As a result of the director's question, I decided to display all professional certifications on the office wall, so there was no doubt in my customer's minds that we were capable.

- As the business changes then your people will need to be able to follow. You cannot be accused by the business of dragging the whole company back because your department lacks the relevant skills. Your team becomes more agile.

- Empowers your staff to get on with their roles without the need for intervention. Some, business as usual tasks require a minimum level of expertise to produce a successful outcome.

- I hesitate to use this word because it has negative undertones these days, but by developing staff, you are "grooming" them for better things – perhaps even to succeed you.

- Reduces the risk of one individual owning all the knowledge and thereby becoming so indispensable that they can hold you to ransom over wage negotiations etc. I have seen this a number of times. These "specialists" have worked their way into a position that is unique and impossible for anyone else to understand. Generally, these people will hold onto all the knowledge – deliberately not sharing it – because it increases their strategic worth. A development programme should help to spread knowledge and mitigate the risk against one person holding all the cards.

- Your team will cultivate a wider (and deeper) knowledge of technical abilities and beneficial business behaviours.

- Your department will have a better track record of delivering on time and within budget.

Forms of Development

Development can be accomplished by direct and indirect means.

The direct approach is quite straightforward:

- Individual professional certifications and qualifications. I learnt a useful lesson a number of years ago about training courses. I had to bring my team of 7 up to speed with their professional certifications. Initially, they would attend a 5 day off-site course and listen to an extremely boring trainer who did nothing more than read from the course book. I couldn't see the added value of enduring the 5 days of tedium, so I looked for an alternative. I managed to find a piece of software that would train the team in advance of taking an exam. The software was a tenth of the price of attending the classroom. My investment was to allow my employees to prepare at home with the software and then take the exam the following Monday morning. These 7 people passed, in total, 30 exams all for under £5,000, which is £166 per exam. The trust you place in your employees is that they will spend a week at home and revise. The quality check you have relates to their pass rate – if they regularly fail the exams then you know they have been playing with the dog all week! You can withdraw development support and funding if this happens.

- Team training courses. There a number of topics that suite group training that don't necessarily relate to professional certifications but should produce other benefits. Aside from the topic of the training course, the group experience provides additional indirect benefits – ie working together or communicating effectively. I have had group training sessions that cover:

- Time Management

  - Six Sigma (Lean)

  - Stress Management

  - Group Profiling (MBTI)

  - Improving Communication

  - Customer Service

  - Be a Better Manager (Why would anyone want to do that?)

The possibilities for group training are only limited by budget and the organisation type you work for.

If you are conscientiously delivering your best managerial experience to your team, then they will be being advanced as a side-effect of their assignments and responsibilities:

- Development by empowerment. When your employees are empowered then they are developing their business skills, self-belief and confidence.

- Delegation. If you offload a task or project to someone else, then you are placing your trust in them to deliver, enhancing their growth.

- Goal Setting and Appraisal. If goals are successful, then the person is growing in the belief in their abilities.

- Brainstorming and Inclusion. An inclusive culture (which includes brainstorming) promotes considered thinking amongst your team and attention to the business and it's goals and how these goals translate into actions.

- Job swapping enhances the understanding of individuals to appreciate different working environments and pressures.

- Team Building enriches the importance of social bonding; better collaboration and clear communication.

On Track?

You can record the progress of your training plans in a lovely template, which will enable you to update your Manager's Dashboard with the progress.

It is highly likely that each person will do more than one training course, but for each, record Course/Certification Name; Scheduled Date; Cost; Complete. These 4 titles will be repeated for every course an individual takes.

It should look like this:

STEP 9 - STAFF DEVELOPMENT

Course 1

Name	Course/Certification Name	Scheduled Date	Cost £	Complete ?
Bonny	Chain Stitch Improvements	01/05/2017	75	Y
Clyde	Chain Stitch Improvements	01/05/2017	75	Y
Jerry	Better Hooking	01/03/2017	100	Y
Eric	Chain Stitch Improvements	01/05/2017	75	Y
Mable	Chain Stitch Improvements	01/05/2017	75	Y
Mack	Chain Stitch Improvements	01/05/2017	75	Y
Dean	Better Communications (Group)	14/06/2017	49	Y
Mr Hancock	Quality Control	05/07/2017	300	Y
Mr James	Quality Control	05/07/2017	300	Y
Mr Hyde	Better Hooking	01/03/2017	100	Y
Mr Wise	Better Hooking	01/03/2017	100	Y
Mr Jekyll	Better Communications (Group)	14/06/2017	49	Y

Course 3

Course/Certification Name	Scheduled Date	Cost £	Complete ?
Time Management (Group)	10/09/2017	92	
Time Management (Group)	10/09/2017	92	
Time Management (Group)	10/09/2017	92	
Time Management (Group)	10/09/2017	92	
Time Management (Group)	10/09/2017	92	
Time Management (Group)	10/09/2017	92	
Time Management (Group)	10/09/2017	92	
Time Management (Group)	10/09/2017	92	
Time Management (Group)	10/09/2017	92	
Time Management (Group)	10/09/2017	92	
Time Management (Group)	10/09/2017	92	
Time Management (Group)	10/09/2017	92	

You can then total up the costs and calculate how progress is doing. The included template provides enough space for 32 staff members doing 4 courses each and calculates all the costs and the teams' progress.

Interesting Asides

I have witnessed some managers suppress their team's tech abilities because they fear they will be surpassed and replaced by a subordinate. If the department is delivering then this is not very likely and is only possible if the department is failing in producing it's deliverables.

Sometimes environmental, technical or legal changes may force development to ensure compliance.

A proper development plan will enhance your department's abilities and efficiency beyond your wildest dreams – so long as you STICK to it (groan).

Template To Use

Training Progress

STEP 10 - COACHING

Browse the internet and you'll find dozens of coaching methods, so which do you choose? There are several very well know ones such as "What is?"; Motivational Interviewing; SUCCESS; STEPPPA, and WHAT – more acronyms than NASA (there's another).

I have tried a few of these and a very popular one called the G.R.O.W model, which I will focus on because it is simple, and it works. You can look this up for yourself, but I have included it here for your convenience and have included some tips to get the most out of it.

Generally speaking, coaching is focused on soft skills and not the operational delivery of a task. There are exceptions of course, but you wouldn't generally use coaching to teach someone how to technically do something, like repair a computer, mend a car, bake a cake or perfect a Larksfoot stitch (I've been surprised at how many exotic crochet stitch names there are. More to come later – contain your excitement) – this would be done in a training or development session.

To give you an idea of what I mean, here are some potential coaching topics:

- To make personal change

- To balance work and family

- To reduce stress

- Taking on a new role

- To find direction and support in transition

- To move forward in something that has been put off for too long

- To have a sounding board and receive feedback
- To get more motivation, and have accountability
- To accomplish something that is important
- To overcome chaos and create a simpler, more organized life
- To improve relationships
- To increase productivity
- To deal with a specific work task
- To deal with a difficult colleague
- Improve Time Management
- Eliminate personal weaknesses

Approaching a Coaching

Crocheting and rhyming – what more do you want?

Your staff should be made aware that you are open for them to ask for coaching at any time. This doesn't mean they can demand coaching sessions ad-hoc – they have to fit your calendar, but they can request a (scheduled) session whenever they like. This conveys the message that their productivity, efficiency and wellbeing are important to you.

You can also promote the coaching opportunity by asking in 1:1's or department meetings if anyone wants some coaching.

The usual approach to coaching is that everything (including the

STEP 10 - COACHING

coaching session) is driven by the coachee, so coaching sessions should be requested by your staff (assuming you have made them fully aware of the availability of coaching sessions – see above paragraph). Occasionally, however, you may spot a relationship problem or a weakness in one of your team members, where some coaching would provide benefits. You have to be careful here – if you bluntly state that someone could do with some coaching, they can take it as a criticism and be an unwilling participant in the session. You have to entice the person into a coaching session (do not use a bag of sweets and a puppy – you could land yourself in all sorts of trouble and has a creepy undertone). This is where you deploy your finely tuned diplomatic skills. The trick is to get the person to realise there is a problem and then want some coaching. The 10ft hurdle here is that most people hold a positive image of themselves and may not recognise there is a problem at all. To jump the hurdle will take time and a lot of gentle probing (figuratively). You could end up spending more time doing this than the actual coaching session. You are coaching someone to do some coaching (this could get complicated). Ask questions in a conversational manner:

How did it go with project Hancock?
How was it working with Mr Wise?
Were there any stumbling blocks on the way?
Did you get held up at any point? What were you waiting for?
How are Bob and Vic getting on?
How's your calendar looking at the moment?
How's your workload?
How's your husband?

These are all questions that should allow you to discover more. Be careful you don't prod too hard as they may twig what you are doing; clam up and you have lost your coaching lead-in. The ambition is to get the person to realise they need some coaching. Even at this point they may not take the final step and ask for a coaching session, so now you can say "Would some coaching help with this?" They are very unlikely to say no.

Skills to Master

Make sure you are there fully. Your presence and inquisitiveness are the most important tools.

Encourage their commitment by being empathetic and showing understanding of the coachee's situation.

Don't go into solution mode.

Blend your questioning style - between very concrete, requiring factual data and abstract questioning to help the coachee with the connection between tangible proofs and traits or behaviours.

Always respect the coachee's opinion by allowing time for them to digest questions and respond accordingly. Don't rush them for an answer.

Be constructive and objective. You don't have to accept everything they say at face value, so be prepared to drill down but remain impartial but positive.

Be in control, clearly state both yours and your coachee's roles and be aware of time (without looking at your watch every 5 minutes).

The GROW Model

Developed in the late 70's this technique has become one of the most widely used, mainly because it is simple, and action and outcome focused.

The coaching session is split into 4 sections called Goal, Reality, Options and Will (although I have also seen the last section called Work or Wrap-up). I prefer the Wrap-up nomenclature.

Throughout the session, you job is to "grease the wheels" by acting as the facilitator and encouraging the coachee to set the goals, outcomes and deadlines with conversational questioning. Remember to remain completely objective and not to slip into solution mode. The coachee needs to come up with the solution so they buy into it.

It is important you set a time limit on the session to ensure you both focus properly. Generally, I have found 1 hour is enough, but you may need 90 minutes for difficult topics. It is widely acknowledged that you should spend most of your time on the Reality section, so a good rule of thumb for the division of time is:

- Goal 15%

- Reality 50%

- Options 25%

- Wrap-up 10%

Tell your coachee of the time allocation to each section, to get them to focus (and not waffle).

Goal

The goal here is to...um...set a goal (3 goals in 10 seconds – better than Man City). Some proponents of GROW suggest that this goal should be a SMART goal (as opposed to a dumb one!) SMART means Specific, Measurable, Attainable, Relevant and Time-Bound. You can have these 5 headings in your coaching template ready to be completed once you have had further discussions in the later sections of the session. I don't believe you can fill in these 5 elements at the start because how can you set specifics and deadlines when you haven't talked the problem through?

Initially then, the goal laid out here should be generic, unmeasured and broad. Remember, this goal should be set by your employee and not you. There is a chance therefore that the goal could be widely unrealistic, and this is ok, because the following section of the discussion, "Reality", will start to define the goal in a more pragmatic way. So, if the coachee says "I want to be CEO in 1 year", just agree and then the discussion in the Reality section will bring the realisation that this is not possible for someone who is 22 with no business training, no previous experience and a degree in the performing arts.

Here are some examples of questions you could ask:

- Can you describe you goal?

- Which concrete change are you aiming for?

- What are your long-term goals?

- Can you briefly explain your issue so that we can set a goal?

- Which subject area do you want to work on?

- Why is this goal/issue up for discussion right now?

- How realistic is the goal?

- Points to remember:

- Be wary of the time – 15% of the total time for the Goal section

- Only allow the definition of 1 goal. If more than 1 goal is defined, then it will be difficult to set the SMART parameters and will be confusing for your employee.

- Remain objective. Although you have to be supportive of your employee, be aware that the discussion may reveal that the root cause of the problem might lie with them. This is more likely to happen if the subject of the discussion is a relationship problem with one of their colleagues.

Reality

This is where you will drive down into the "realities" of the situation using 50% of the session time. Your questions will be probing in order to gain a real-world description of the issue or goal defined. Find out what is going on and examine the present situation to gain a detailed view. It is tempting to start discussing solutions here but try to hold off on this until the next section

Try to discover:

- Who first detected that there is an issue?
- On a scale of 1-10, how much does this situation bother you?
- When and how often does it happen?
- What are the consequences of the present situation?
- Who else is affected by the situation?
- Who else is involved in the situation?
- How much influence do you have over the situation?
- Who else has influence over the situation and how much?
- Does the situation represent an opportunity or a problem?
- What do your colleagues think about the situation or problem area?
- Has anybody done anything to change the problem before?
- Which distinct hurdles are to be surmounted?
- What would Eric do in your position?

- If you were me, what would you do?

- Who knows about your aspiration to change the situation?

- What responsibility would you like to have in the present situation?

- Do you have any training needs in order to accomplish the goal?

Options

By now you will probably have come up with more than one possible options. This section is to choose one and start to flesh out the specifics and deliverables to accomplish the goal – ie some of the SMART parameters will start to form.

Your role is to stimulate the coachee into developing their own ideas and certainly not to provide them with solutions. Work towards ensuring that choices are made and prioritised.

Running through the following questions will help determine the specifics:

- What are the possible options you have to resolve the situation?

- Are you ready to choose a solution?

- Are there alternatives to the ones you have mentioned? Think outside of the box.

- Which solution do you prefer and why?

- Is your preferred solution the one that provides the best result?

- What can you do to change the situation?

- Whose other standpoints would be relevant?

- Have you seen comparable solutions applied elsewhere?

- What are the strengths and weaknesses of your various options?

- If your problem was solved now, how would the situation be?

- If you do not take action now, what will the situation be in 6 months?

- If you were to share your situation with your colleagues, how would they react?

- How realistic is your option on a scale from 1-10?

- Do you need help and if so how do you get it?

- Do you want to hear some of my potential solutions?

- Are there any external factors that could affect the success of this goal?

- How do you know when you have attained your goal?

- What are the measurable factors of the goal accomplishment?

- Who else should be involved?

- How long will it take?

Wrap-Up

This should be the easiest and quickest section to complete if you have worked through the other sections properly. Go into action mode (solutions at last!) and gain commitment from your employee.

It is important to set the following:

- What are they going to do?

- Set a concrete and specific action plan.

- Determine what, how, and when.

- Identify hindrances and a clarification of requirements.

- Ensure commitment and follow-up.

Running through the following questions will help determine the specifics:

- How do we ensure you stay motivated?

- What would reaching your goals do for you?

- What actions can you do immediately?

- To what extent does the plan achieve your goal?

- What could prevent you from reaching your goals?

- What are your criteria of success?

- Do you have any personal resistance to initiating the tasks?

STEP 10 - COACHING

- What are you going to do to surmount the obstacles?

- Which resources do you need to reach your goal?

- Who needs to be informed?

- What will you do to get the support and when?

- When shall the goal be accomplished? Is it realistic?

- What impact do your actions have for your colleagues?

- Does the completion of the goal fit your attitudes and values?

- How committed are you to realise these actions? On a scale from 1-10?

- If not 10, what is the reason?

- What can I do to support you?

In essence, you set actions, ensure commitment and schedule a review.

At the end of this section, all your SMART parameters should be complete, so let's review what SMART is here:

Specific. This is one of the few times in life when it's good to be narrow-minded. Zero in on the specific action that results in the goal success. If you have ended up with a goal that is very broad like "Improve my performance" then it's too broad and you'll have to start again!!

Measurable. How will you measure the success of the goal? You should be able to quantify the success. Statements like "Improve inter-departmental relations" is not a measurable statement. Much better to have "Reduce inter-department arguments by 50% in 4 months". It's not always possible to assign some numbers, but it is possible to assign a measurable metric. If you can't think of a way of measuring the success of the goal, then your goal is too broad, and you have to start again!

Attainable. Clearly, the guy who can't tie his own show laces but wants to be CEO in 6 months, apart from being mildly deluded, has an unachievable goal. The goal must be pragmatic with the constraints of planet earth. You cannot blow your whole budget on a single person; they cannot become world champion crocheter if they are allergic to wool.

Be realistic – the goal should be achievable in respect of:

- The person's abilities
- The current level of business activity
- Your budget
- Time allowed
- The availability of others to help.

Relevant. I have experienced employees asking for coaching sessions only to realise their goal is to do something that is completely irrelevant to the department and/or company. One employee wanted some training in a completely different subject than his current role – it turned out he wanted a career change and was hoping the company would help him on his way. From his perspective, it was worth a try I suppose.

The goal must be relevant to the person's role and your department.

Time –Bound. Having an open-ended goal means one thig – it won't get done. Setting an explicit deadline will focus energies and makes the scheduling of a review possible (you must review, otherwise you won't be able to check on progress or success). When setting the deadline, keep in mind the "Attainable" ethos – if the deadline is too tight, then your coachee will probably fail and the whole value of coaching will be lost.

Template To Use

Coaching Template

STEP 11 - CONVERTING COMPANY GOALS INTO ACTIONS

Every now and again, your company will come up with a new set of high level strategic goals (commonly this takes place when there is a new CEO).

These might be:

1. Improve the EBIT (profit)

2. Improve the customer satisfaction

3. Enhance company security

Some departments will have a direct connection to these goals and will therefore enjoy the focus of resources to help them deliver. So, the directly connected departments in these examples would be:

1. Improve the EBIT – Finance, Production, Sales

2. Increase customer satisfaction – Sales, Marketing, Production

3. Enhance company security – Facilities, IT

Because of the extra attention these "directly connected" departments receive, then translating high level goals into actions should be relatively straight forward. Your company will no doubt have it's own way of achieving this, but there is a definition of the steps required below, which you should find useful.

What if you run a department that is NOT directly connected to one of the strategic goals? It is common place for managers, in these cases, to struggle with the concept of how their department can contribute because there is no discernible correlation between their department and the defined goals. With a little thought and effort, these departments can contribute, although the outputs might have an indirect influence on the strategic goals.

Gerry runs the IT Department. How does he contribute to Improved EBIT?

Lewis runs the Finance Department. How do they contribute towards improved customer satisfaction?

Bonny (apart from being an expert crocheter. Hooked yet?) runs the Marketing Department. How do they contribute towards improved company security?

For an easy life, a lot of manager's answers to these questions will be "I can't contribute, so I won't bother trying". Bear with me, it is possible but don't expect a 100% success rate. Just to make matters more difficult, your upper management will probably not include you in their plans for some of the goals because they themselves cannot see how your department could contribute. If this is the case, your department will not have been included in the communication waterfall. You will therefore find yourself in the dark about the initiatives set out by the higher goals. Your only option is to go and ask, stating your intentions to try and contribute to all goals even though there is no apparent link between your departments function and some of the goals. Be prepared to stand your corner on this – some superiors will need convincing of the gains to be had. Be determined, however, because there are 2 potential paybacks. 1 – You will raise your profile (don't be afraid to put your head above the parapet – only occasionally will your head be shot off. Predominantly you will gain from this behaviour, so long as you bandage your head regularly). 2 – It is likely that your department will be in the minority (of 1) to be actively endeavouring to impact on company goals, so you will be a trailblazer.

Now you will have another issue that you probably won't be able to resolve. Even if you convince your superiors that your department can contribute to all goals, it is doubtful that you will be allocated any more resources or money. You therefore have to do what you can with your existing resources.

You discovered that your superiors needed some influencing to see the connection between the stated strategic goals and your department's potential contributions. Now you have another group to inspire – your team. Initially, it is very likely that they also won't see the connections either, so how do you get their buy-in to ensure their full support? Brainstorming. I have written a separate chapter on this, so I won't go into that here. Suffice to say, you have to do some initial preparation before your brainstorming session. This first question to ask yourself is "Can my department really positively contribute towards the goal stated?" Specifically, what outcomes are you expecting? You may decide that it is impossible (sometimes it is). How does an IT department help to improve the company's customer satisfaction? An option is to skew the goal to fit what you can deliver. In the IT example, you could define the customer as your internal customers, focusing on the departments that are directly connected to the strategic goals. So, how could you improve your delivery to the Sales department, who are focusing on the "Improve Customer Satisfaction" goal. By improving your service to them, you are indirectly helping with the end goal.

There are 6 steps during the brainstorming session and one after it. Start at the top of your whiteboard with step 1 – each subsequent step gets written below the previous one. Each step is a breakdown or outcome from the previous step

1. Write Down The Strategic Goal. Write it at the top of your whiteboard – the team needs to be reminded of the goal they are working towards.

2. Strategic Goal Initiatives. The individual tasked with leading the project for each strategic goal will have (should have) broken the goal down into some high-level initiatives. Before the brainstorming session, you should have done some detective work to find out what these are. If you are skewing the goal to fit your department then your team will have to come up with these (although some preparation in advance by yourself will help with this too). How can the high level goal be separated out into initiatives? There should be maximum of 5.

3. Initiatives Success Factors. What factors will determine the effectiveness of the initiative? The success factors should be generic, arbitrary statements (i.e. no KPIs) that define the elements that are required for success. Some examples – For improved customer satisfaction, one success factor might be "improved communication". For an improved ebit, one success factor might be "make equipment last longer". Notice these are worded statements – they do not include actual measurements (such as KPIs). The success factors help to channel the focus in determining what tasks need to be done.

4. Define your actions. You can now use your initiatives and success factors to cultivate actions or tasks that will be allocated to individuals or groups. In essence, this is the process of breaking down your initiatives into something that can be physically delivered. Each initiative could produce between 2 and 5 tasks. If initiatives are resulting in more than 5 tasks, you need to separate the imitative out into two.

5. Set KPIs or Other Measure of Success. Only when you reach level 5 can you define specific targets or KPIS. Be careful not to overestimate or tie yourself into unrealistic targets. It is highly probable that you will have to revise these at the review stage.

6. Allocate Resources. If you have the workloads of your team at hand then you may be able to allocate roles here, which will improve buy-in if they are encouraged to volunteer.

A sanity check is required here – will you be able to deliver? Based on your knowledge of your team's workloads, is there some unused capacity? Only you and your team can decide this. You may have to reprioritise other projects or tasks. What is the impact of delivering towards strategic goals? Is the impact greater or less than some of your existing projects or tasks? How easy is it to achieve? If you define a new action which has a low impact on the strategic goals and is difficult to implement, then is it worth doing?

Remember to assign tasks to people with the correct skills. Ie don't ask someone to come up with some tasty designs for new leaflets if they can't even draw a stick man. (Definitely don't ask me – I'm the only person I know who can make a stick man look overweight. Useless!)

You can use your project/task evaluation tool to help you decide.

7. Review and Repeat. Goal posts change, people take holidays, a full moon happens once a month and companies can change their mind, so plan for change and change the plan. It is not uncommon for initiatives to be scrapped, tasks to be reallocated or for KPIS to be altered to suit. If, after review you change a KPI figure from 90% to 5%, then you were clearly over excited in the brainstorming session! You can review the progress of the tasks in the same way as you review everything else – 1:1s, department meetings, 90 day plan reviews or a special session to ask, "How are we progressing towards the Strategic Goals?"

Templates To Use

Project or Task Evaluation Tool

Converting Strategic Goals into Actions Template

STEP 12 - RETAIN YOUR STAFF

If you find that the only way to retain staff is by tying them to their chair, then you probably need to go back to chapter 1.

All of these aspects - office is too warm/cold/noisy/quiet; workload is too high; too few holidays; pension is poor and even a low salary are not the sole reasons that people look for another job. Indeed, a person will tolerate a number of these factors before looking for the "greener grass". There is one single factor though that can (and often does) lead to employees getting another job – A BAD MANAGER!

I have friends who have done this because they just couldn't endure the bad boss's behaviour any more. When one steps back and thinks about that, it's incredible the impact that one person can have. Imagine the loss of time and effort spent recruiting the departing staff - and the cost! People can dread the thought of going to work and some are even scared by their inconsistent and vindictive manager.

Recruiting is time consuming, stressful and costly, so make sure you retain the staff you recruit. There isn't one thing to do – it's a combination of delivering on all your managerial promises thus:

- Choose the right team in the first place by asking the business what business behaviours it wants to see and then selecting someone who fits those behaviours but also has a good fit technically with the role they will do.

- Ensure that coaching sessions, 1:1's and department meetings are all hosted regularly – with few cancellations.

- Safeguarding the staff development plan

- Delegating properly without intervention. This empowers your people.

- Being engaged with your people without micro-managing

- Asking for reverse feedback (you shouldn't be worried by this).

- Guaranteeing no bombshells in the yearly appraisal.

- Exploiting your staff skills fully. If you explore this, you will be amazed at what they can do.

- Diligent goal setting and quarterly plan creation with follow up.

- Some team building breaks down social barriers and enhances team cohesion.

- A culture of inclusion. 2 heads are better than one so getting your team to contribute their ideas as much as possible.

- Properly recorded career aspirations that you actively support.

- Demonstrating all the good manager behaviours and exhibiting none of the bad ones!

- Some miscellaneous other factors you can consider – can they work from home? Is flexitime possible? This is all about work-life balance, which employees place a high value on.

- Endorsing equal opportunities. No favouritism.

- Cakes or donuts on a Friday morning? Christmas quiz (usually held around December).

- Celebrating successes. My team once completed an office move into a large office. I had a custom cake made with the Microsoft Windows logo printed on it (with edible ink). It didn't cost much, but made the day special and a break from the norm. Small gestures go a long way.

- Be realistic. Most people don't live for work but work to live. Within these realism boundaries, try to make work as engaging and enjoyable as possible

There will be some factors such as salary, working environment, bonus and sometimes career development that may be out of your complete control – you simply have to do the best you can within your jurisdiction.

Being a high quality manager will reinforce your employees trust and respect and massively help to retain them. There is also the added benefit of your department delivering more because the engagement from your people will be enhanced.

In a large company I worked for, career development for my team was limited due to geographical limitations. Against this backdrop, over nearly 10 years, I achieved 100% staff retention. Don't misunderstand – I happily ejected the "flies in my ointment", but nobody left by their own choice. This was accomplished in part because I "walked the walk" and didn't just "talk the talk" – ie I delivered the best possible managerial experience for my staff. I know I am blowing my own trumpet here, but as stated earlier, celebrate your successes. It should validate in your mind that I have earned the right to describe all these management techniques because they are verified by results in the work place.

STEP 13 - BRAINSTORMING

2 heads are better than 1 right? Well 6 or 10 heads are even better. Brainstorming can deliver a wealth of valuable (and unexpected) ideas to transform into actions, as well as nurturing an inclusive and collaborative culture in your team.

What do you brainstorm? The philosophy is open, so you can brainstorm anything. You can even set up a session to brainstorm "What do we need to brainstorm?" – this can bring to light the weaknesses in your department that need improvement. The point is, there are no restrictions.

So, what do you need? Open minds, post-it notes, a whiteboard and plenty of chocolate biscuits. Although brainstorming is meant to provide a free, open discussion, where nothing is discounted, you have to be careful it doesn't result in a melee of voices with no productive outcomes. Thus, it's important to create a structure and set some rules to ensure your staff get the most out of it.

Your "stormers" must be clear about the purpose of the session, so you need to define a topic beforehand and, this is important, is relevant to them and their skillsets. If your company makes luxury cars, you can't ask your IT people to improve the power output of your V12s!!

The Whiteboard Guru

This person will run the whiteboard and ensure everyone sticks to the rules. It's a good time to give someone in your department a small development opportunity, so you, as the manager, just become one of the "stormers". Everyone should be given the chance to be the guru at some point, but clearly their skillset and personality are important. You can't thrust the role on someone who is shy and dyslexic – this would cause too much stress and wouldn't lead to an efficient session. The guru also has to recognise that they mustn't be biased towards their own ideas. If you end up with a whiteboard full of the guru's ideas and nobody else's then something has gone wrong and it's cost a fortune in chocolate biscuits.

The Note Taker

Unless you are lucky enough to have someone who can do shorthand, it can be difficult for a note taker to keep up with the whiteboard as the ideas flow in. A good idea here, is to photograph the whiteboard and then document the results after the session.

Set Some Ground Rules

You want to deliver some actions, so it's important to avoid the mayhem we see at Prime Minsiter's question time. Laying out the ground rules will encourage fruitful discussions and real actions:

Set the Level of Detail. You don't want to get into implementation plans or costings or any other low-level detail of each idea. The session is about exploring potential concepts that can be looked at in detail later. The whiteboard guru needs to be able to identify when discussions are getting into too much detail and move on to the next topic.

Interruptions are not allowed. It's ok for people to ask for clarifications but members should be allowed to speak without interruption. Another responsibility of the guru here.

Objectivity is Vital. "Stormers" will be passionate about their own ideas to the point of being unrealistically biased in favour of their own ideas. It's important then to remain objective throughout the exercise.

Everyone gets a chance to speak. Your quieter members will not naturally push their ideas forward, so ensure they are given a slot.

Basic Structure

Your session will be time bound – probably between 1 and 3 hours. Like a good book, your session should have a suitable beginning, middle and end.

In the Beginning. Before the meeting, determine what the topic is and what the expected outcomes are. At the start of the session, review the ground rules and let everyone know what the whiteboard guru and note taker will be doing. The guru should now start their brain cells working by asking everyone to write the topic at the top of an A4 piece of paper and then write ideas on to post-it notes and stick them on their A4. This is called single brainstorming. A combination of individual's ideas and group ideas will be most successful. Your quieter employees will find this time their most productive and rewarding – not everyone enjoys debating. 10 minutes should be a minimum amount of time allowed for this.

Middle Spread. Most of your scheduled time will be consumed here (and the chocolate biscuits). The guru writes down all ideas on the board and initiates the discussion of each. Each contributor should be asked to talk about their own ideas. You and your guru have to keep a watch on the clock, because time can quickly evaporate during the dialog. Some ideas will disappear from the board and some new ones added. Safeguard the ground rules throughout.

The Payoff. Probably the most important section of your session. Assess the factors that affect the implementation of the ideas.

Rate each idea for:

- The value to your department and the business on a scale of 1-5. 1=low value, 5=high value

- The resources needed, such as manpower, costs etc on a scale of 1 to 5. 1=high resources, 5=low resources

- How difficult is it to implement bearing in mind the resources required and other factors such as collaborating with other departments, organisation structure and politics. 1=Difficult, 5=Easy

Plot these values in a spreadsheet and then sort them with the highest total score to the top. You can then set the priority of each idea. See table below:

Idea	Priority	Value 1-5 1=Low, 5=High	Resources 1-5 1=High, 5=Low	Difficulty 1-5 1=High, 5=Low	Total Score
Idea B	1	5	4	4	13
Idea D	2	2	4	5	11
Idea A	3	3	3	2	8
Idea C	3	3	1	4	8
Idea E	5	1	1	3	5

You can decide later who will take on the work of implementing.

Some Known Techniques

There is a wealth of brainstorming practices on the internet. These methods are helpful for producing objective results. I would be nice to play with all the techniques, but the brainstorming session is not a laboratory for trying out all the differing styles of brainstorming. If you try too many, then your sessions will overrun, and output will be reduced. I have listed some here, but it would be sensible to cherry pick just one or two for each session:

Figuring Storming. Ask your "stormers" to put themselves in the shoes of others. Perhaps the group of people who will be impacted most by an idea. Also wise (from your career standpoint) is to do this in your bosses shoes, and his boss, and what the hell, the CEO.

Mind The Gap. You are at point A and want to get to point B. Write down the steps to bridge the two.

Change Your Attributes. Your "stormers" should change 1 thing about themselves – their race, gender, language, nationality, culture etc. This will stimulate new results and different perspectives.

Reverse Storming. Playing devil's advocate can be beneficial but you have to be conscious of the pitfalls. Your members can become discouraged if their ideas seem to be being overly criticised. Channelled correctly, this technique will identify potential obstacles and therefore solutions to ideas.

Introduce Roadblocks. Add some ridiculous constrictions to the mix. How would you rollout this idea with a budget of £10? What can be done by this time tomorrow? All documentation needs to be in 5 languages, including Clingon (I promise that one of your geek employees will do it!). Stormers can find this difficult but it can invigorate creativity

Remove Roadblocks. Your stormers will be unwittingly thinking within the boundaries of your organisation. They are definitely thinking inside the box - remove the restrictions. What if there was an unlimited budget and resources? Don't worry about politics or organisation structures. There are no limitations. This can be fun and deliver an abundance of ideas, some of which will be crazy, but there will be some golden nuggets in there too.

When It's All Over

There is no point in doing any brainstorming if no actions and deliverables arise from it. Your note taker needs to get busy and document the outputs and then staff need to be assigned to each idea. It's wise of course to allocate the work to the originator of the idea because they will fully believe in it. Farther down the line, as with any target set, the progress and success of the idea need to be reviewed.

I'm off to buy some shares in McVities.

Template To Use

Brainstorming Ideas Evaluation

STEP 14 - QUARTERLY PLANS

Why?

It may be that your employees are happy working their fingers to the bone doing 1000's of chain stitches daily, but it is more likely that they are looking for something different and more challenging, such as some lacy shell popcorn stitches? What could be more exciting?

Most people will relish something to relieve the monotony of "business as usual" duties. You will find that they will jump at the chance to do something different. In fact, there are some people who will do "anything" else rather than deliver a useful product, so be watchful of these. In point of fact, the larger an organisation gets, the more of these "unproductive floaters" you get. Personally (and from what friends tell me), there are quite a number of these types who generate one question amongst colleagues..." What do they do?"

Assuming then that your team are all delivering their BAU tasks, then providing an opportunity to be involved in something more challenging and rewarding is you delivering (to your team):

- Staff development

- Good quality delegation

- Goal Setting

- Appraisal opening

- Staff empowerment

A quarterly plan grants employees the prospect of setting some longer-term goals and deliverables.

What they can be used for

I can't set out specific ideas for the plans, suffice to say, they are generally long-term work that should last about…erm, a quarter! This means that the work should (in general) last no longer than a quarter and be a minimum of 6-8 projected weeks. Sometimes there will be work that will last longer than three months and that's ok, just use the quarterly plan process and extend the deadlines to suite.

By and large, the ideas for quarterly plans will emanate from:

- Already defined projects that have come from the business

- Outputs from brainstorming sessions, which you could host purely for the reason of getting some quarterly plan ideas. I have done this, and it is surprising how creative a bunch of people can be even with a blank canvass.

- Outputs from sessions for converting strategic goals into actions

- Outputs from department meetings

- Projects or long-term improvements that you define based on your projected department deliverables for the year. I.e. one of your KPIs might be to improve customer satisfaction by 5% which can translate into one or more quarterly plans

- Staff Development. Normally I wouldn't use a quarterly plan for staff development as these are covered elsewhere in your planning. However, there may be times (such as just after recruiting someone) when they have a lot to catch up on to get them up to the same speed as everyone else, in which case, you could use a quarterly plan.

Plans Overview

From all the sources that define potential quarterly plans, you should list them to monitor their progress. Not all plans can begin immediately depending on workloads etc, but they should be recorded so that they can be looked into when resources allow.

For this, you can create a table with the following information:

- Task. A helicopter view of the quarterly plan.

- Outcomes. What is the desired result?

- Main Driver. Who is the main person responsible for the plan?

- Team Members. Who else on your team is involved?

- Resources. What other resources are required (customers, suppliers, other colleagues).

- Dependencies. What dependencies will affect the plan result? If the plan is to produce crocheted blankets 30% quicker, then will this depend on your yarn supplier delivering daily? Can your supplier achieve this? If not, then your whole plan may be scuppered.

- Start Date. This could be a potential start date for a plan due to start in the future and based on your known workloads, schedules and resources available.

- Completion Date. Again, this could be a proposed completion date for plans to start in the future.

- Progress. A percentage out of 100. This makes it very easy to get an overview of progress in Excel.

25 EASY STEPS TO PEOPLE MANAGEMENT

You should end up with a table like this:

Plan	Sub Tasks	Outcomes	Main Driver	Team Members	Resources	Dependencies	Start Date	Completion Date	Progress
Quicker Crocheted Blankets	Daily yarn deliveries	Produce 30% quicker	Sid Hancock	Dawn S	Long Yarn Ltd	Long Yarn Ltd	01/11/2016	22/01/2017	25
	Improved stitching patterns			HR					
	24/7 shifts			Production					
Customer Satisfaction	Reduce complaints	Improve by 25%	Tony James	Jennifer F	Production		01/04/2017	01/07/2017	0
	Improve quality			IT					
	Improve our response times			Marketing					
Reduce the use of the word governance	Promote the use of other words	Decrease of 90%	Ronnie B	Ronnie C	Rogets Thesaurus		01/04/2016	15/05/2016	100

Control and Recording

For 'control' I should have used the word governance, but that word is a pet hate of mine. I know it's only a word, so how can it irritate me? It's one of the words that you constantly hear from people trying to sound professional. "Governance for this", "governance for that" – it's like they swallowed a management glossary and wanted to make the most of it.

To ensure your quarterly plans are successful and deliver on time you need some governance (oh fcuk!), I mean control. You probably know by now that I love templates (some could say this is because I am lazy, but I like consistency and templates offer this). So, create a template with the headings shown below. You should then organise a session to discuss and complete the template with the relevant staff member.

Quarterly Plan Template

Here are the headings for your template:

Objective

- Description. What is the goal? Describe the overall plan and any sub-tasks along with the outputs for these.

- Success Measures. How will you know if the plan is successful? A quarterly plan is a form of goal setting, so ensure you define it within the SMART parameters – ie the goal should be Specific, Measurable, Attainable, Realistic and Time Bound.

- Deadline. Set a start and end date.

Responsibilities

- Main Driver(s). Some quarterly plans may involve more than one team member, but it is a good idea to assign somebody as the main driver to ensure accountability. The main driver will propel the plan forward and ensure the documentation (the template…. yay!) is updated.

- Additional Resources. Who are the other team members? Do you need to describe their involvement?

Resources

- Budget. Not all quarterly plans will add to budget, but if any unusual costs are to be incurred then note them here. The main driver has to ensure they keep within this budget.

- Other resources (suppliers, external colleagues).

Control and Communication

- Scheduled Meeting structure for team members. How often do the quarterly plan team need to meet?

- Schedule to update manager. When do you need to be updated on the plan progress?

Progress

- Activity log with dates. Set this out as a table so you can record all sub-task activity, with these column headings:

    - Who? – Who did the sub-task?

- Sub-task – What is the task?

- Start Date

- Completion Date

Review

- Achieved Result. What was the outcome? Did the achieved result match the initial goal of the plan?

- Lessons Learned. Anything of value learned along the way? This will be particularly useful if the desired outcome was not achieved. Is this is the case then why? What hurdles prevented the desired outcome?

- Success Rating. Give the plan a score for effectiveness – I would suggest a percentage out of 100. This measure is useful in a number of ways:

  - You can use it to add to your Managers Dashboard to assess the success ratings of the goals being set.

  - Your employee can add to their logbook as a milestone event, which will expedite the yearly appraisal.

Summary

Aside from all the juicy managerial opportunities as mentioned above, you really will be offering some real-world developments opportunities to your employees. These opportunities will maximise your staff potential and is all part of retaining a successful team. Once last task for you is to ensure that quarterly plans and their success are discussed openly with the whole team in the departmental meeting or in a dedicated review.

But the main question to ask is did you get those blankets out quicker without the use of the G word? (I can't say it – I just can't...because I have good governance.... oh sh**!)

Templates To Use

Quarterly Plans Overview

Quarterly Plan Template

STEP 15 - EMPOWER YOUR STAFF

If your employee's chairs are wired to the electricity supply, then you have misunderstood. Empowering staff and delegation are closely related but it is worth briefly touching on the topic as there are some additional aspects to consider

Delegation is a sub-task of the overall philosophy of empowering your staff. There is one question to ask about staff empowerment. Do employees have the authority to carry out their work without the need to constantly get approval from their manager? Included in this authority is the ability to make decisions independently.

Are Your Staff Empowered?

There are a number of symptoms that will help you assess if your staff are empowered.

Symptoms of poor empowerment:

- You are regularly involved in delivering the output of your department.

- Your workload is dramatically larger than your team members.

- Your department regularly fails to deliver on time and within budget.

- Your team are not always pulling in the same direction.

- You regularly get asked if it is ok to do something.

- You find that work has frequently stalled because people don't take the decisions.

- You have to intervene in people's work.

- People don't volunteer to take work on.

- You spend quite some time quality checking what your employees produce.

- In 360° reviews and employee survey results, your ratings are low. This is because your employees don't respect you for not trusting them.

That's the dark side, so here are the indicators that your staff are properly empowered:

- Your team deliver the output of your department. You could be occasionally involved if there is a big push on something, like a rush order.

- You only get asked to make a decision about the direction to take occasionally. For "business as usual" work, people asking you to make a decision is a rare occurrence. For some major decisions, perhaps connected to a project, you are sometimes involved in making the crucial decision.

- Everyone has a fair workload.

- Your department surpasses KPIs and delivers on time and in budget.

- Work progresses smoothly and does not stall.

- You are not intervening in peoples work.

- People are "self-starters". They come to work and just get on with it.

- Employees volunteer to undertake more work because they trust you to let them work without intrusion.

- Your 360° or employee survey results are encouraging, which indicates your staff appreciate being empowered.

Some Points To Remember

- For projects, especially with an inexperienced person, it may be worthwhile setting some constraints on what decisions can be made without referencing you – such as a budget constraint. This is to ensure that mistakes are not made with major decisions. If the person has plenty of experience, then they should be able to make these decisions personally.

- Let people learn from their mistakes, with feedback from you.

- Don't expect all delegated tasks to be completed to 100% of your satisfaction. Staff have to learn what you want. Are you being pedantic? If you did the task, would you deliver to the standard you have set? Don't set standards that you can't achieve yourself.

- With appropriate feedback, then people should improve each time they do some work or a project. You need to monitor the performance and assess whether improvements are being made. If there is no improvement, then this needs to be addressed.

- If you complete the delegation rating template, if will provide a good indicator if you are empowering your staff or not.

- Celebrate success. Personnel don't just want more money as the only way to show appreciation. Realistically, you can't give money away every time somebody achieves a target. People want to be appreciated for their industry and a simple thank you goes a long way.

Time to unwire the chairs?

STEP 16 - FULLY EXPLOIT YOUR STAFF SKILLS

Did you know that Clyde, your maintenance technician, is a Scout leader in his spare time? Bonny, your office administrator, is an expert crocheter and does watercolour painting too? Are these extra-curricular interests any use to you as the manager? You bet they are.

As the manager, it isn't good enough for your department just to deliver on it's KPIs. There is a high chance that your organisation won't have spelled out to you clearly what they are expecting in addition to the KPI delivery. There is also a high possibility that they haven't even thought about it. If your department can deliver extra, even if you haven't been asked to, your profile will be raised. Don't be afraid to publicise your successes, although hiring a small plane to tow a banner showing how good you are may be going too far.

So how can your staff's untapped skills help towards you, ultimately, being promoted? Continuous improvement. Every department can improve the efficiency and effectiveness of what they do. Most people relish the opportunity to show what they can do, especially if it is something outside of their normal job remit where they can demonstrate their expertise.

Collect Your Talents

Firstly, we need to found out all the talents in your department. I would suggest doing this individually with staff in 1:1s. Some people are poor at promoting themselves, so privacy is important to encourage them to divulge. The best approach is honesty, so tell them why you want to know - that you intend to give people the ability to take on more interesting tasks, use their talents and raise their profile. One point to consider - some people don't like revealing anything about their private life, so you can't push it. Another shortcoming, which you can help to overcome, is folks' inability to remember what they are good at or like. How many CV's do you see where the hobbies are reading, travelling and socialising? It can't be true, people are doing more things than this.

Type in "list of Hobbies" into a well know search engine (no product placement here!) and you can easily get a list of hobbies to copy into Word (oops, product placement). Print this out as a prompt sheet to help your team remember what they do – they will surprise themselves. When they have finished, you need to ask them if they will mind you showing their hobbies, interests and skills to the rest of the group.

Once you have finished your talent scouting, record the results in your employee skills matrix. Now organise a group session to brainstorm how you fit the talents to some tasks.

Match Your Talents to Tasks

Before the group sessions, you should have a go at coming up with some tasks (improvements) for your department – these will act as a starting point to get your teams creative juices flowing. Fake it till you make it, right?

Begin the session by stating the required outputs. You want to improve your department's efficiency by setting up a continuous improvement program utilising all the talents the team has. State that it will provide an opportunity to do something interesting, rewarding and fruitful.

Show your list of tasks and ask for input for new suggestions. I would plan for this taking up half the time you have allotted (which should be an absolute minimum of an hour). Make a note of all suggestions.

Now display the groups talents (remembering to respect the privacy of individuals) and declare that the job now is to match tasks with pertinent talents (skills).

Here are a few examples of harmonising tasks to talents:

Task to Skills Cross Check

Task	Hobby/Interest	Skill Used
New Intranet Page/Website	Artist/Writer	Artistic flair, Good Grammar
Instructional Videos	Actor	Confidence, Projection of Voice
Data Analysis/Charts	Fantasy Football Player	Analysis, Attention to Detail
Improve Office Environment	Gardener/Interior Design	Knows about air quality, enjoys efficient use of space
After Work Exercise Classes	Tennis Player	Fitness, Coaching
Office Move	Football Coach	Organising
Redecorating the Office	Artist/Interior Design	Understands colours, space etc
Christmas Party	Scout leader	Organising Events
Tidy Maintenance Bay	Stamp Collector	Fastidious
New Documentation	Avid Reader/Writer	Good Grammar and linguistics

The second half of the session now matches the correct skills to the tasks. Buy-in is an important factor here, so it is prudent to promote the idea of staff members choosing their own tasks based on their skills. You have to ensure that they really are eager for a task based on their skills and not just because the task sounds the most interesting. You gain nothing if the wrong talents are applied to tasks. There should be a lot of discussion in this section and all should be encouraged to contribute so pay special attention to the quieter ones. Be watchful of team members not being given the chance to work on a task that suites them – some egos could get bruised, so joint task work is fine (after all, it will nurture collaboration).

After all that, some target dates need to be set and of course the tasks progress has to be reviewed.

A remarkable side-effect of properly assigned tasks is that you shouldn't find yourself having to chase them up. Your staff will be self-starters because it gives them an opportunity to utilise their expertise and ultimately shine.

Going forward, ideas for new tasks will materialise and it will be simple to assign them based on your team's skills. Your role is to be vigilant of workloads – there should be an equal and fair spread of workloads, otherwise the task success rate will fall and your KPI delivery also. After all, Bonny doesn't want to be so overworked that she has no time for crocheting!

Templates To Use

Skills Matrix Template

Task to Skills Template

STEP 17 - SKILLS MATRIX

Which of your people can do a Catherine wheel stitch and how many years' experience? I'm going to guess that, in reality, 99% of you will answer none. I will also guess that the same 99% are getting "needled" by my crocheting theme.

Creating a skills matrix is relatively simple task and provides:

1. A complete list of all your staff experiences, qualifications and education.

2. Helps you to spot training requirements to ensure your staff development program continues.

3. Improves the matching of people's skills to new tasks or projects.

The skills matrix is best kept in the form of a table to assist in analysis and is particularly helpful if you have a large team. Create a spreadsheet with the following columns:

- Name

- Country (if appropriate)

- Role

- No. years of experience

- The primary work area in the last 5 years

- Level of education

- Diploma/degree or masters title

- Professional Qualifications. All industry sectors have professional qualifications.

Allow 10 columns to allow people to record up to 10 professional qualifications.

Send this spreadsheet out to all staff and get them to complete it. You simply then copy all the results into a master version for easy reference. See the Skills Matrix Template – it has the results for 56 fake people and is based on IT employees.

The Analysis

Your master spreadsheet will be able to provide the following overviews:

Qualifications

You should get a count of how many people have certain qualifications, like this

Qualifications	
MCP	23
MCDST	8
MCSA	9
MCSE	5
MCITP	3
Novell	2
CCNA	6
CCNP	1
CCIP	1
CompTIA A+	4
CompTIA Network	2
	0
SAP	0
SQL	1
SUN	0
UNIX	1
	0
Prince2	2
Apple	1
ITIL Foundation	29

You can also get a list of all people with a certain qualification:

Qualification Checker
MCDST
Ava Ingram
Billy Morrison
Jennifer Jenkins
Lara Carroll
Lily Kaur
Nicholas Rowe
Noah Haynes
Zak Whitehead

Last 5 Years' Experience

In what roles have people been working in the last 5 years?

Last 5 Years Experience

Role	Count
IT Support	34
Server	11
Network	10
Exchange	5
Lotus	2
SQL	2
Database	1
User Admin	3
VBA	1
Citrix	1
Concorde	1
SUN	0
UNIX	1
System Administrator	1
Domain Admin	2
	0
	0
	0
	0
	0

Level of Education

For reference only really, but useful to know:

Level of Education	
Degree	24
Diploma	20
Apprenticeship	9

Who Does What?

You can have a search function that list all people doing the same role:

Who Does What?

IT Support

Abbie Day	21
Adam Marshall	3
Andrew Rhodes	7
Ava Ingram	12
Billy Morrison	6.5
Bradley Whitehead	5
Brooke Jenkins	9
Brooke Murphy	10
Daisy Matthews	8
Declan Haynes	3.5
Ellis Newman	9
Emily O'Neill	7
Ewan Matthews	1
Gabriel Connolly	2
Harry Ingram	11
Henry Waters	15
Jack Matthews	1
Jordan Kaur	9
Joseph Coates	5
Josh Hanson	1.5

Combine 2 Overviews.

Of particular importance is to look for gaps in staff development (including missing qualifications). This is easily done by reviewing the list of people doing one function alongside a list of people that have a pertinent qualification. In this example, the list of people are all IT Supporters. MCDST is a Microsoft qualification for supporting desktop PCs. For a good quality delivery of IT Support, all of the team should take the MCDST qualification. You can see from the example below that less than half the team have taken the MCDST qualification, so you can include this in their development program.

Who Does What?

IT Support

Abbie Day	21
Adam Marshall	3
Andrew Rhodes	7
Ava Ingram	12
Billy Morrison	6.5
Bradley Whitehead	5
Brooke Jenkins	9
Brooke Murphy	10
Daisy Matthews	8
Declan Haynes	3.5
Ellis Newman	9
Emily O'Neill	7
Ewan Matthews	1
Gabriel Connolly	2
Harry Ingram	11
Henry Waters	15
Jack Matthews	1
Jordan Kaur	9
Joseph Coates	5
Josh Hanson	15

Qualification Checker

MCDST

Ava Ingram
Billy Morrison
Jennifer Jenkins
Lara Carroll
Lily Kaur
Nicholas Rowe
Noah Haynes
Zak Whitehead

Template To Use

Skills Matrix Template

STEP 18 - STAFF LOGBOOKS

Off the top of your head, can you remember how Ginger performed against KPIs this year? Can you remember how Eric's project went? More to the point, can they?

The honest answer is that you and your staff will remember <u>some</u> of it. Unfortunately, it is likely you will both remember different things, which can damage your standing with your staff because they will believe they are right and you haven't "paid enough attention" over the year. If you have gaps in your knowledge, your employees <u>will</u> know which is not good for your reputation.

Plugging these gaps will greatly improve your knowledge and help to build a trusting relationship.

Why Have Logbooks?

You and your employees won't have to rely on memory which can be fogged by too much coffee, time going by, stress, company machinations and of course age. If everything is recorded in a log, then your memory can metaphorically put it's feet up. The real benefits are reaped when it comes to the yearly appraisal. Remember that there should be no surprises for your employees at a yearly appraisal – they should have an accurate perception of how they are performing throughout the year. Going into a yearly appraisal with gaps in your knowledge of their achievements could be embarrassing at best and morally damaging for your employee at worst.

The Content

The principle of the logbook is to record everything of merit and importance regularly, so the likely inclusions will be:

- Milestone Achievements such as the success of Projects, Quarterly Plans and Other Tasks.

- KPI Performance. You should be in a position to provide these stats monthly to your employee at their 1:1

- 1:1 Discussions and Outputs. 1:1s will inevitably lead to actions and outputs which should be bullet pointed in the logbook. Included in this feedback should be a monthly appraisal score (based on the same scale as your organisation's yearly appraisal ratings).

- 360° Review Results

- Profiling Results such as MBTI or Thomas International

- Development Plan Progress. Are they on track? Is some more focus required?

- Any other milestone output or result from any meeting with yourself or the department.

Each category should be recorded under it's own titled section in the book for ease of reference later. So the headings would be as the bullet points above.

What's the Format?

The choice here is a compromise between convenience and security. An A5 notebook with say 100 (ish) pages is a simple and convenient way to record everything during the year. It's great advantage is that it is easy to update because it is "at hand" – "on the fly" notations can be added easily. A word of caution here – It is likely the logbook will contain the individual's performance against KPIs, 360° Review results, profiling outputs and 1:1 content and no doubt the book will be left lying around occasionally. This literally could become an "open book" with some employee espionage - colleagues won't be able to resist having a quick look at their team mates book, so privacy is blown away.

The more secure but less convenient option is to create an electronic logbook that can be protected by passwords and/or storing it in a permissions-based folder. For a logbook to have any value then it must be consistent and updated devotedly otherwise it will start to resemble a Swiss cheese and nobody likes a cheesy book. This is certainly more arduous in an electronic format since your employee will have to be at a computer and staunchly update it after a 1:1, department meeting, appraisal etc. There is a potential for them to forget, so it is important to remind them of the logbook's value if this behaviour crops up.

Your Commitment

Initially, your staff may not understand the value of the logbook or why it benefits them, and it does impose a small administrative overhead (which nobody enjoys). You will need to be persuasive and encouraging at the beginning – selling the virtues of the logbook principle.

If you can manage to get "buy in" then you have to ensure you are committed too by ensuring you go to meetings with all the performance results prepared – ie KPI stats, appraisal scores, project success rates etc

Extra Benefit

Over a few years, your employee will gain a better understanding of their achievements, certifications, innate skills (and weaknesses) and ratings and how all these stats relate to their general performance and growth.

Extra Extra Benefit

It's almost impossible for one person to remember all the pertinent facts and figures about a group of people. Unless you are Mr Memory (or Mrs) then you will forget which could be insulting to your staff if they see you don't "know them". Plug those holes with a log book. Additionally, the logbook will help with your decisions about staff development, skills assessments, promotion candidates because an employee's skills (hard and soft), their accountability, work ethic, character traits and performance will all be readily available in the logbook. It will also help to answer other questions. Is the person growing? Are they helpful? Do they go beyond the call of duty?

The logbook becomes an informal resume and aide-memoire to ensure you know your team members and their potential. Trust and respect will be nurtured as your staff will see your commitment to them (so make sure you prepare. Remember the old saying Prepare to Fail by Failing to Prepare).

By the way, Ginger glided through her KPI stats and Eric's project "Morecambe" was a great success bringing a lot of sunshine to all.

STEP 19 - TEAMBUILDING (WITHOUT OIL DRUMS AND PLANKS)

You know, I have never built a bridge out of oil drums and planks in my life – I feel left out. I wish I had been on more teambuilding events. What I have noticed is that larger companies do more of this, probably due to that extra spare cash sloshing about. Small companies don't do much teambuilding at all, but interestingly, have an innate team ethic due to their small size. A company with 5 employees will naturally be more cohesive than a large corporation because they are physically closer and tend to know everyone and everything that is going on.

Actually, it's ok not to do teambuilding if you think your team is "well gelled" already. However, for most people working in larger SMEs and bigger, some well thought through teambuilding can have dramatic positive results on the department.

Humans have a tendency to be "glass half empty" about the unknown, especially in the competitive working world. I have witnessed dozens of examples of staff members coming up with negative perceptions of others, without any evidence as backup. Regularly this perception is factually wrong and stems mainly from people not knowing each other well enough. It's much easier to be critical of someone you don't know. The foundation of all department performance is good inter-inter-personal (as opposed to intra-inter-personal – get me? Probably not) relations. Put simpler, people have to know each other – their families; their hobbies; interests; family history etc. Be aware, you cannot force anybody to divulge information about themselves – some people are more private than others. Generally though, taking the staff out for a meal or a drink (not during working hours of course) will break all those social barriers and lay the first stone of the team's foundations. This may sound like I'm stating the bleeding obvious, but you would be surprised at the number of managers who don't even get this. I'm afraid the working world is full of bad managers.

Everyone loves a jolly right? If your company can afford it then these are great social barrier breakers. Some competition in the department is healthy, but just be aware that a "competitive" jolly could cause some small riffs. If you have two highly competitive people then put them together as a pair, so they work as a team rather than against each other. As time goes on and their relationship strengthens, you can experiment to see how they perform on opposing teams. Interestingly this will provide insights into their behaviours and could form part of a future development plan if you spot weaknesses. You should use teambuilding as an opportunity to observe your staff but don't walk round with a clipboard making comments or noises like "mm, interesting" or "uh-huh". If the staff know they are being observed, then they will act differently and not relish the event fully (it's essential your staff should enjoy themselves). There are oodles of competitive "jolly" events like off-road driving, clay pigeon shooting, karting, bowling and golf. Non-competitive activities are possible, but not as prevalent to buy on the internet. You could go for a hike; fly sports kites; team crocheting or fishing (you have to know that all team members are prepared to push a hook through a maggot).

Although jollies are fun and have some social use, they don't require your staff to work together (a team!) to deliver something.

I have played a number of paper based or verbal teambuilding games. Although interesting, I don't believe they deliver a positive experience. In most of the games, the team will fail because the games don't have enough instructions and you have to get into the mind-set of the creator, which is impossible. Usually, teams learn of their failings afterwards and how they should have done it differently, which is not a positive reinforcer. I once did a day out driving various quick cars. One instructor spent his whole time telling us that we were missing the apex, braking and accelerating at the wrong point etc etc. In essence he just criticised without telling us how to do it properly (I think he had a whole bag of chips on his shoulder because his racing career had come down to showing novices how to drive round an airfield!). Another instructor was brilliant – an older, laid back, guy, who just told us how to go quicker. Everyone enjoyed that experience more than any of the other instructors.

I once took my team to a recording studio, which was surprisingly cheap. Their task was to write the song and lyrics, play the instruments and record the song in 3 days. Initially they were daunted because none of them played instruments (that's why I chose it), but it didn't take long before they were helping each other with their chosen tasks. Ultimately, they learnt a lot about how to work together, had a great time and had a (admittedly quite bad) song they could take away.

Teambuilding should push people's comfort barrier, but within reason. You can't expect someone to abseil down The Shard if they have vertigo and certainly don't enter your team into the next marathon if they are predominantly donut eaters.

The best (and cheapest) way of teambuilding is at work. Every organisation can provide opportunities for groups to come together to produce a useful outcome and build the team dynamic. One of the most fruitful ways is to get people involved in a project outside of their normal job remit because they will relish the opportunity to do something different. Does the office need re-painting? Create a vegetable patch (we did this). Reorganise the office. Setup a cost saving scheme.

During my time as an IT Manager for a large corporation, we had to install the IT equipment and move staff into new offices over a dozen times. I used this as a perfect opportunity to team build. I would bring in the whole team to work over a weekend (and I never had any complaints about this), work long days to a set plan and then socialise in the evening. The only cost to the company was accommodation and meals, which was cost effective because the job had to be done anyway. The sense of camaraderie was high and resulted in a fruitful, productive outcome. The team bonds were strengthened in the long term and I could watch my staff behaviours (without a clipboard!).

STEP 20 - JOB SWAPPING

Variety is the spice of life right? Well, for most people, but not all. I once got a Christmas job where I had to check the accuracy of spirit level vials. The vial is the plastic bit that has the bubble in it. I had to clamp each vial into a holder that had a light source at one side projecting the image of the bubble onto a white piece of card. I then had to put feeler gauges under each end to test the accuracy of the bubble. Hundreds a day.... sooo boring. After 2 days I was almost brain dead. The guy who ran the bubble checking team had been doing it for nearly 40 years!!! I don't know how he put up with that level of tedious repetition for so long unless he was in a rock band at the weekends or went bungee jumping every night.

The majority of (normal) people will look to enhance their working life. This can be achieved by job swapping.

What's the Point?

North by North West (if you like a bit of Hitchcock).

Job Swapping for your team provides:

- Development opportunities.

- Increased awareness of their peer's workload, environment, customers and pressures.

- Chances to reduce or eradicate misconceptions about how others work.

- A change of scene.

- New experiences that they may be able to use back in their own office.

- A degree of upskilling.

It is quite understandable that different departments build virtual walls, sometimes called silos. Bigger organisations spend some time and money to ensure that these silos are broken down to help departments communicate freely and openly. It is also possible for virtual walls to go up in the same department, especially if they are geographically spread, leading to the misconceptions of each physical group of people by the other. I have witnessed this. Even though both groups of people are decent, self-starting hard workers, they perceive their peers at the other location to be lazy, having more fun and where their grass is markedly greener. I got around this once by installing a large video-conference screen that permanently displayed the other office. Colleagues at both locations could simply turn in their seat and talk to someone at the other end. Their understanding of each other's workload, pressures and customers led to a dramatic reduction in misperceptions and an improved team dynamic.

Video conference systems are expensive and nothing is as good as the personal touch, so job swapping is a much improved method of improving your team spirit and all pulling in the same direction.

There are two forms of job swapping:

1. Doing the same job but in a different location especially if the new location is Prague, Barbados or even Bilston if you are really lucky (look it up).

2. Doing a different job but in the same location (or a different one....mm, that's 3 forms)

Same Job Different Location

If you have a team that is spread over a number of locations and your staff generally all have the same function, then this type of job swapping is the easiest to achieve. You shouldn't have to be concerned whether your job swappers are technically possible to swap for a short while. After all, processing an invoice is the same in the UK and Singapore.

Your only major limitation on this type is by the budget.

Different Job Same Location

Common sense is the byword here. It would be a bad decision to job swap a Lathe Operator and a Production Director because their technical abilities are so different. Be realistic about your choice then, the job swappers have to have roles with a similar level of expertise. This doesn't mean that job swapping of this type doesn't have any value – it does. These staff members may do different roles even though they have the same technical ability.

However, because of the capability constraint, this type of job swapping is more difficult to achieve but is still possible.

Something to be observant about – there may be some resistance from one or both of the parties as they see the other person's role as subordinate or lesser than their own. This needs to be overcome by driving home the importance of knowledge sharing – working as a team, transparency etc.

Customer Job Swapping

I know I said there were only two "real" forms of job swapping, but there this third type which is more of a customer relations and awareness exercise.

It is often the case that one department will depend on the outputs of another department before it can proceed. Regularly this relationship can cultivate misperceptions especially if the receiving department believes it is being let down by the sending one.

Customer job swapping can help to raise the understanding of how the other department functions. Pragmatically, these will be non-productive in terms of deliverables – the job swappers will not be able to do the others work because there will be such a difference in roles. It is worth noting here though because these types of job swaps can reduce misconceptions and build relations between the two teams, which should help with future efficiencies.

Who to Swap

Your employees doing the same job but at different locations? No brainer, do it.

Are there some roles that are not exactly the same but have similarities? Could a small amount of training permit cross fertilisation of people?

Whoever you chose, ensure that over the year, everyone gets an equal chance to swap. If Mr Martin gets to job swap to Barbados twice a year, while Mr Lewis swaps once with the Skelmersdale office then that's not fair is it? I mean, Mr Martin will be so envious. No favouritism from a good manager.

Regularity

This has nothing to do with your employee's toilet habits.

Essentially you should job swap while it can produce useful outcomes and the budget allows. It would be wise to add something into your budget for job swapping because it is a very effective way of developing staff and increasing team efficiency. Evidently, if you team is spread across the world then the expense of travelling will constrain your opportunities.

One-way job swapping is useful to provide extra cover for maternity/paternity; holiday cover or special events, like moving into a new office.

Remember that job swapping should only take place over a few days (a week at the most) unless you have extraordinary circumstances. If people swap for longer than that then you might have to start re-writing job descriptions!

STEP 20 - JOB SWAPPING

Record It

Setting up a simple table of who has swapped and when will show the number of resources swapped and help to plan going forward.

You should end up with this:

	Job Swappers					Person Summary	
	Name	Duration (Days)	Name	Duration (Days)		Name	Duration
Jan	Mr Hancock	3	Bonny	3		Bonny	11
Feb	Jerry	2	Mable	2		Jerry	10
Mar	Mr James	4	Ronnie C	4		Mable	8
Apr	Mr Hancock	2	Ronnie B	2		Mack	6
May	Mack	4	Mable	4		Dean	7
Jun	Mr Wise	1	Bonny	1		Mr Hancock	11
Jul	Jerry	3	Ronnie C	3		Mr James	11
Aug	Mr Hancock	6	Ronnie B	6		Ronnie B	8
Sep	Mr Wise	2	Mable	2		Mr Wise	3
Oct	Jerry	5	Dean	5		Ronnie C	7
Nov	Mr James	7	Bonny	7		An Other	0
Dec	Mack	2	Dean	2		An Other	0
		41		41			82

Use the Person Summary to look out for inequalities in job swapping.

Anyone want to swap with the guy doing the spirit level checking? Thought not.

Template To Use

Job Swapping Template

STEP 21 - 360° DEGREE REVIEWS

There are numerous methods for people to appraise each other:

Channel	Feedback Provided
1:1s	Manager to Staff and Vice Versa
Yearly Appraisal	Manager to Staff
Employee Survey	Staff to Manager

So, what other useful feedback loops are there, that are not included in the above 3?

- Self-Rating. How good do you think you are? (Brilliant, no doubt). How good do your staff think they are? (Even better than you!!). Even if you are a realist, there will be times when your perception of your abilities is out of line with the perception of your staff or your manager. This doesn't mean that you will always overrate yourself – there will be times when your team and/or your manger perceive a certain ability of yours to be better than you think.

- Peer to Peer. Employees rating their peers - and other managers (at the same level in the organisation) rating you.

- Customers – Customer surveys are common in companies but nearly always focus on external customers. What about internal customers?

A 360° Review will enable all of these 6 feedback types in one channel and is the only place that employees can get a rating from their peers. The additional benefit is that all the results can be analysed in one place.

360° reviews then are not only very useful for your employees, but just as valuable for yourself because it is your only opportunity to gain opinions from customers and other managers.

Sometimes Anonymous

In your team, if Eric thinks that Ernie doesn't deliver then Ernie needs to know, but NOT that Eric thinks it. People don't like criticism even if it is warranted and constructive in nature. Peer to Peer ratings and employees rating their manager MUST remain anonymous, which presents challenges when it comes to reviewing and discussing the results later.

There are 2 occasions when anonymity isn't possible:

1. If your team only has 1 member! Is this really a team? More of a duet really.

2. Your manager rates you. I assume you know who your manager is!

There is nothing you can do about this. My experience is that any ratings given in these 2 situations are polite, rather than a true reflection.

Survey Channels

You could hire an amphitheatre, dress as Russel Crowe, shout out your survey questions in a Roman/Australian accent and get your respondents to give a thumbs up or down, but you'll be down the job centre quicker than your sandals can carry you.

In these days where so many things are preceded with an "e" or "i" to show they are ecological or intelligent, you surely need to use an electronic from to gather ratings. I once had a boss in the noughties who decided on a paper-based survey with cardboard collection boxes. I didn't work well – people don't like writing things anymore, but it did give us a good selection of paperclips and chewing gum

The 3 "e" key techniques are:

- Word document. Easy to set the layout and write the questions but has two big drawbacks:

  - Difficult to set up validation on the answers. If the answer needs to be in a range of 1-5, how do you ensure that Word only accepts a value in that range? I'm sure some Word gurus could do this but it's way over my head.

  - Collating results. Getting all the results into one place for analysis can be tedious if you are collecting results in Word.

- Spreadsheet. The big advantages here are that data validation is relatively easy (so you can ensure the answers are within the ranges you set) and collating all the answers into one place for analysis is easy. To ensure anonymity, you must send people (by email) their own spreadsheet to complete – you cannot share a link to a common spreadsheet as people will be able to read what others have done.

- Online survey. You may have an IT department that can this up for you, but from personal experience, I have setup a number of online surveys myself using one of the free surveying tools available on the internet. Once you have created the survey, you just email the link to your potential respondents. All respondents' answers are invisible to others. There is a very well-known survey tool called Survey Monkey, which is very capable, but only allows 10 questions and 100 responses free – if you want more than that, then you have to pay. My choice is Google Forms because it is totally free, without any limits on questions or responses. The only pre-requisite, is that you will need to have a Gmail account. It also has other useful features such as:

- All the results are automatically collated into an online spreadsheet that you can download.

- All Google Forms are mobile friendly, so respondents can use their tablet or smartphone.

- All entries can be validated to ensure your replies have the right values.

The 3 Groups to Ask

Each of the 3 groups to survey can result in potentially 6 sets of results:

Group	You	Your Staff
Peer to Peer	From Other Managers Equal in Position	Review Each Other
Manager (Up and Down)	From Your Manager and From Your Staff	From You
Customer	From Customers	From Customers

Who is Reviewed?

On the surface this looks complicated and you certainly don't want your respondents to go into "survey burnout" but actually you only need 3 sets of different questions:

1. Manager Questions. The questions will be focused on managerial skills. You can send this question set out to your manager, your managerial peers and your staff.

2. Staff Questions. The questions will be focused on delivery, technical skills and staff behaviours towards the rest of the team. This question set is sent out to your staff only.

3. Customer Questions. The questions will be focused on knowing and satisfying customers. This question set is sent out to customers only but can be used to review yourself and your staff.

Your will need to send a separate set of invites for everyone that needs to be reviewed (including yourself). If using Google forms, you will need a separate form for each person being reviewed – this keeps the results for each reviewee separated and not all mixed together in an unmanageable dump of data.

The Survey Questions

When designing the questions for your staff and customer groups, you may need to tailor them to suite whatever your business does, whereas the questions for a good manager should be the same regardless of the organisation.

It is relatively easy to come up with 30-40 questions for each group, which may seem too many, but if the survey is written correctly, it should only take 5-6 minutes to answer these questions. The knack here is to write questions that require a numeric rating from a scale of say 1-5 and avoid questions that need wordy answers. Defining questions that only need numeric answers also greatly speeds up collation and analysis and reduces the possibility of mis-interpretation.

The Self-Analysis portion of the 360° review is extremely important because it allows the reviewee to measure how they perceive themselves against the ratings of others. To maintain anonymity, you cannot ask for someone's name as one of the survey questions, so how do you separate the reviewee's self-ratings from those of others? Your first question needs to ascertain this as such:

> Q1. In relation to the person your are reviewing, you are:
>
> 1. That Person
>
> 2. Their Manager
>
> 3. Managed by Them

This will enable you to easily identify your self-ratings, Managers, Customers, Peers and Staff who work for you.

The full list of questions is visible in the 360° Review Template, but for your convenience here is the Top Ten for each:

Manager Questions

Manager Questions (Peer to Peer & Manager To Staff)
How do I effectively set objectives and prioritise tasks?
How well do I involve staff in setting their own objectives
To what extent do I coach and develop on technical expertise?
I ensure that appraisals are constructive in nature to improve performance
How well do I build and retain a team
I Communicate company goals to subordinates
I create a team culture based on company values
How well do I meet targets schedule and budget.
I devise and manage clear long and short-term goals
How well do I demonstrate an understanding of the company goals
I connect operational plans to the company goals

Staff Questions

Staff Questions (Peer to Peer)
Helps and cooperates with other team members to get results
Contributes ideas to improve team effectiveness
Takes action to settle problems quickly
Communication skills.
Is Service minded
Will take action to improve under performance
Is Trustworthy
Correctly prioritises work
Works in a structured manner
Is a Team Player

Customer Questions

Customer Questions (For Manager and Staff)
Develops high quality deliverables
Understands the customer's business and needs.
Communication skills.
Is Service minded
Is Cooperative
Correctly prioritises work
Is Organised

Two important points to remember:

1. If the review is about you, then do the survey yourself and be honest – take my word for it, you are not brilliant at everything! Comparing your self-perspective with that of your boss and your staff is extremely useful – it forms part of your self-development plan.

2. In the rating scale (choose whatever scale you like but make it numeric because it is easy to analyse later) include a "N/A or Don't Know" option because some questions don't necessarily relate to everyone.

The Results Are In

Collate your self-ratings, your manager's and your staff answers alongside each question. Is your boss out of line with what your staff think of you? Does your boss generally rate you lower or higher than your staff? If it is the former, why? Are you out performing him/her? Do they feel threatened by your performance? It may be something as simple as you have not been good enough at celebrating your successes – i.e. your boss doesn't know how well you and your team are doing. Make sure you and your team's successes are recognised.

There will be one set of results for yourself and a set of results for every member of your team, but the analysis is fairly straightforward.

Your Results

You will have sent the survey out to your staff; your manager; your peers and, of course, answered the survey yourself (about yourself). Because of the (vital) question 1, you will easily be able to distinguish the answers from your answers; those of your manager; those of your peers and those of your staff. Your top left-hand corner of your table should look like this:

Date and Time	Are you The Person, Their Manager, Manged by Them, Their Peer
04/11/2013 02:55	That Person
04/11/2013 02:56	Managed By Them
04/11/2013 02:56	Managed By Them
04/11/2013 02:57	Their Peer
04/11/2013 05:57	Their Peer
04/11/2013 09:08	Their Peer
04/11/2013 09:19	Their Manager
04/11/2013 10:12	Managed By Them
05/11/2013 14:34	Managed By Them

If you have used Google Forms, then your responses are automatically posted in a spreadsheet with the questions across the top (the columns) and the responses listed down the side (the rows). You can add your calculations, such as average score, top 5 results, bottom 5 results and the big variances between your self-ratings and those of your manager and staff.

If you have stuck to predominantly numeric ratings then analysing the results in a spreadsheet is simple, including some useful extracts:

1. What is the reviewee's average score? If your scale is based on 1-5, if you have someone who has an average of 1.5, then there is clearly a lot of work to do with this person in many aspects of their behaviour or delivery. This "someone" could be you!! Someone with a high average is clearly well appreciated by their peers, customers and yourself – this is an employee to take note of (especially if your own review has a low average ☺. Your successor is in the room?)

2. The reviewee's top 5 and bottom 5 results. Focusing on remedies for the bottom 5 should produce results with the biggest impact for the least amount of effort. The low hanging fruit, as they say.

3. The reviewee's blind spots. These are the scores where their self-rating is markedly different from everyone else's. If someone has consistently marked themselves highly then there is a strong possibility that they have an overrated self-opinion and won't give a damn that others have a lower opinion. Conversely, receiving higher ratings than the self-rating is moral boosting for anyone.

Discuss the Results

One of the primary ways of becoming a better manager is to get feedback from your people. Finding out your weak points and improving on them is vital, so reverse feedback is an essential (if a somewhat scary) technique to employ. A lot of managers never ask for reverse feedback because they are scared what they will hear, but, so long as your staff remain professional, hearing how well you are doing is extremely constructive. Your 360° review results then are a great opportunity to discuss your performance. You should organise a session to review your results and discuss:

- Your strengths – Your Top 5 results. There is nothing wrong with highlighting what you are good at.

- Your weaknesses – Your bottom 5 results. You really need to understand what improvements you need to make.

- Your negative blind spots. For what survey questions are your "self-ratings" much higher than your staff? There could be a number of reasons for this:

    - You are a bit of a big head. Being as polite as possible – do you have an overinflated opinion of yourself?

    - If you manage a small team and you have 1 employee who is not particularly happy about something and have given you low scores, then the impact on the average result is great. They could be unhappy about any number of issues that are not necessarily connected with your managerial prowess. They may want more money; to be able to work flexitime; have some personal issues etc

    - The question has been interpreted differently. I have experienced this – a somewhat obvious question to me has been interpreted differently by other people.

- Your positive blind spots. If your "self-rating" results are markedly lower than your employees then you are doing well by their standards, but you may to be being too humble about your achievements.

Your long-term aim is to ensure that you achieve above average results and that your staff agree with your "self-ratings".

To respect people's privacy, you cannot discuss each of your team member's results in an open forum with the rest of the team. Use their

360° results as the basis for discussion in 1:1's, appraisals and to lead to possible coaching sessions.

PS. All the survey questions have to be about professional behaviours and attitudes – nothing personal. So, you cannot add a question "Does Ernie have short fat hairy legs?" even if it's true and Eric is desperate to answer it.

Template To Use

360° Review Template

STEP 22 - BALANCING WORKLOADS

Has Mr Jekyll seemed unapproachable recently? Has Mr James regularly reported in sick? Did you hear Jerry & Dean (normally very good colleagues) at each other's throat last week?

There could be a myriad of reasons for these uncharacteristic behaviours including illness, personal problems and the wrong type of yarn (crocheters love a good yarn), so don't assume anything. It's the manager's job to provide a balanced and fair environment including individual's workloads. If workloads are uneven then the examples above could be a symptom. If you record and review workloads on a regular basis then you can eliminate the worry that your employee's behaviour is not down to a biased, unjust division of labour.

What to Record

The principle is to set a value against any kind of work that your team are doing. By adding up all their values and comparing them to other employees, you can see if the work split is reasonable. You record values for:

- Business as Usual (BAU) work. How much work is required to complete service calls or process the invoices or bake the cakes?

- Project Work. Some projects may be a joint effort involving more than one of your team. You may have a project lead and an assistant – their respective workloads don't have to match.

- Tasks. These are like miniature projects but will ultimately require some work.

- Special Duties. This is work that may not get measured with KPIs or other appraisal scales, but nevertheless somebody has to do it. E.g. Bonny has to gather KPI stats each week or Clyde has to stock the fridge with milk every day. There could be loads of very small tasks here, so to keep life simple, you could collate all these into one value to cover all.

- Anything else that creates some kind of workload for the employee. You could include any personal development work, ie training. I know this is not strictly work (or a department output), but the person will have some work associated with the training.

How to Measure

Use a simple scale (this is not a scale of how simple you are!) of say 1-10 (I use 1-5), where 1 = Low Workload and 5= High Workload.

Make a preliminary assessment yourself for each of their BAU, Project, Tasks and Special Duty work. You can then discuss this with each team member (individually or as a group) – be prepared to amend your assessment because you may not have fully understood the work involved.

There is an interesting observation to take note of here – staff will err on the high side when assessing their own workloads – i.e. they will regularly assess workloads to be higher than your initial thoughts. This is the natural (competitive) nature of humans – they want to show you and their colleagues that they are "very busy". Reviewing workloads as a group will typically reduce this "over assessment" because it is more difficult to pull the wool over the team's eyes than one over-worked manager (Not you of course, because you have everything under control, right? ☺).

How to Record

A well-known spreadsheet that excels in summarising numbers.

The first tab will be a summary of all the workloads from all the areas of work already mentioned. The values here will be automatically calculated from the other tabs in the spreadsheet where you record the actual workload values.

STEP 22 - BALANCING WORKLOADS

So, the summary would look like this:

Live Workloads

	BAU	Special Duties	Tasks	Projects	Other	Total	% of Total
Bonny	4	4	2	5	1	16	7%
Clyde	4	6	5	4	3	22	9%
Jerry	5	6	7	5	3	26	11%
Eric	7	4	4	4	3	22	9%
Mable	5	4	0	3	5	17	7%
Mack	4	2	0	6	4	16	7%
Dean	8	15	6	7	5	41	17%
Mr Hancock	5	6	3	6	3	23	9%
Mr James	2	0	7	4	5	18	7%
Mr Hyde	3	5	0	3	1	12	5%
Mr Wise	2	4	6	5	1	18	7%
Mr Jekyll	2	5	0	3	5	15	6%

You then create a tab for each of the work areas, so – BAU, Special Duties, Tasks, Projects, Other – 1 tab for each.

In each of these tabs you record the specific work and its workload value.

For BAU, it could be:

BAU Work

Who	BAU 1 Description	Workl	BAU 2 Description	Workl	BAU 3 Description	Workload	Total
Bonny	Phone Support	3	Ticket Answering	1			4
Clyde	Phone SUpport	1	Ticket Answering	3			4
Jerry	Ticket Answering	4	Phone Support	1			5
Eric	Invoice Processing	3	Supplier Quotes	3	Phone Support	1	7
Mable	Supplier Quotes	1	Stock Control	2	Invoice Processing	2	5
Mack	1:1s	1	Stock Control	1	HR Liaison	2	4
Dean	Customer Liaison	4	Customer Quotes	4			8
Mr Hancock	Manager Assistance	1	Payroll	2	Job Distribution	2	5
Mr James		2					2
Mr Hyde		1		1		1	3
Mr Wise		2					2
Mr Jekyll		2					2

Your summary tab, will demonstrate if there is a workload equilibrium. Clearly in this example, Mr Jekyll and My Hyde need to spend less time in self-reflection and get some work done!! You can also see that Dean has the highest workload – maybe that's why there is tension with Jerry?

Share and Share Alike

There are a number of advantages of reviewing the department's workload as a group:

1. As already mentioned, team members will be more "realistic" with their workload assessment in front of colleagues

2. You will be selling your "socialist" endeavours for a fair working environment. Your staff will see that you take their workloads seriously and there is no favouritism.

3. Sometimes it is unavoidable that someone has a bigger workload than others (a big project roll out for example). By openly sharing the workloads, you have given an opportunity for staff members to volunteer to help out those with bigger workloads. In the event that nobody steps into the breach, you can volunteer someone (the art of delegation). This has also provided you with an assessment potential in observing the levels of selfishness, selflessness, team spirit, individualism etc.

Initially, you will have some extra work to do – creating the spreadsheet and then listing and evaluating the workloads. Going forward though, it is a relatively painless task to update the numbers once a month to ensure you stay on track. From numerous surveys I have seen, one key measurement of a boss (from an employee's standpoint) centres around the question of "How well does your boss understand your daily work?" You will genuinely gain a better understanding of your department's daily operations by logging and appraising workloads. You will also validate (openly) that you are diligently working towards a proletarian utopia!! Well, that's perhaps going a bit far – let's just say you will earn some social currency (hmph, it used to be called brownie points in my day ☹).

As for Mr James, well his workload isn't too high, so there maybe something else going on there....and guess who has to find out? Good luck Sherlock.

Template To Use

Workload Calculator

STEP 23 - REVERSE FEEDBACK

If you have ever watched Top Gear, you will know that their reverse feedback is to say "you're alright, you're alright" while somebody reverses a truck (and as is usual with Top Gear, until the driver hits something!)

Reverse feedback is not a replacement for parking sensors, it is the (sometimes scary) tactic of asking your staff how you could do better. As with the 1:1, where employees get some quality time with their manager, reverse feedback is a quality opportunity for you to learn how to be a better manager.

In actual fact, I never found reverse feedback to be scary at all – I welcomed any opportunity to improve my delivery to my staff. However, some managers are so worried about what they could hear that they shy away from reverse feedback and hence miss the chance to improve. There is a strong possibility that these managers know they are not delivering an acceptable level of managerial provision.

You can get appraisals from your staff via 360° reviews; employee surveys and in 1:1s. 360° reviews and employee surveys will tend to result in a number-based rating – ie a score out of 5 or 10. This is great but doesn't go into details of specifics. Reverse Feedback affords the possibility of receiving feedback in words and anecdotal evidence or examples of when you could have done better.

You will gain great strength in admitting your weaknesses. If you don't know your weaknesses, then how can you improve on them?

Repeated Coercement

Reverse feedback is a relatively new idea. Managers certainly didn't ask staff to comment on their performance in the 80s and 90s – if they had, the employee would have requested their union rep was present!

So, people are not comfortable with the idea of telling their boss what they think of them. Well of course, some folks are, - they take great pleasure in it, but for most of us, it's an uncomfortable request.

When you start asking for feedback, the net effect could be disappointing. Here are some of the reasons and suggestions to improve the quality of what you hear:

- Staff are worried about "comeback" from their boss about the things they say or they are concerned about their career potential in your department. You have to state clearly (and repeatedly) that you welcome the feedback and that there will be no negative repercussions from yourself. Keep reaffirming that's its ok for staff to give feedback. My team members took a while, as it was new to them.

- Staff do not realise the significance of the reverse feedback to you. Make it clear that you value the feedback highly as it is your opportunity to learn to be a better manager for them. You should state that it is your aim to be the best manager you can, and you need their help in achieving it.

Reverse feedback should be conducted face to face, which makes the situation even more unsettling for the team member. The face to face element is extremely important as it permits a good discussion; examples to be given and for you to assess the validity of the persons comments.

Because of all these reasons, your first few feedbacks may consist mainly of answers like "erm, yes good" and that's all.

To increase the value of the feedback you receive, provide a list of topics that your team can think about.

Reverse Feedback Topic List

You really have to control what people are allowed to mention as it can decline into a whinging session. This is especially true if you have been struggling to gel your department or are new to the role.

You also need to prompt people to talk, so a topic list has two benefits:

1. It helps people to think of topics to give feedback on

2. It prevents the feedback straying into unprofessional territory – like your choice to wear Dame Edna Everage glasses. A strange choice, but it is YOUR choice and is off the table for reverse feedback.

I have found that staff will not always bring the topic list with them to the meeting, or indeed, have done any preparation in advance.

Two actions required:

1. Email them the topic list before the reverse feedback session and say that their feedback is very important to you as it enables you to become a better manager and therefore they will benefit from that. Ask them to prepare specific examples if they can, because this will provide useful evidence of how you are doing. In reality, this is extremely useful to you because it will enable you to assess the example and decide whether it is a legitimate example of where you could do better or is the real issue lying elsewhere, like a problem between 2 employees.

2. Print off and take the topic list with you to the meeting.

The topic list covers the 6 main managerial deliverables and behaviours.

The topic list is meant to be an aide memoire to start conversations. It is not a survey, so employees don't (and should not) speak about every question shown on the template. They should cherry pick the subjects that they feel they need to bring to your attention.

Here is what to have on your topic list, grouped by the 6 main managerial deliverables and behaviours:

Goal Setting

- How do I effectively set objectives and follow up?

- How well do I involve staff in setting their own objectives?

- I ensure that staff have objectives on whose success they have significant impact

- I ensure that staff understand task prioritisation

- I devise and manage clear long and short-term goals

Delegation and Follow Up

- Do I delegate tasks?

- Do I support you in your work without taking ownership of the work?

- Do I have follow up conversations?

- Do I provide enough feedback on your progress for work?

Coach & Develop

- Do I lead through questions rather than merely providing answers?

- Do I use conversations as opportunities for development through coaching?

- Do I contribute to the development of your technical expertise?

- Do I provide support to help you improve your performance?

Appraise

- Do I ensure that you have a clear understanding of your performance level?

- Do I provide regular feedback?

- Do I ensure that all appraisals are used constructively to improve performance or expertise?

- Am I aware of the wishes you have for future job content?

Choose & Retain a Team

- Do I select and retain staff who contribute well to overall team performance?

- Do I take the tough path and proactively replace staff that do not contribute consistently?

- Do I communicate and create a high level of team spirit and engagement?

- Do you have open and constructive dialogue with me?

General Behaviours

- How willing am I to change my decision for the benefit of the organization?

- I foster an open and trusting environment

- How are my communication skills?

- I create a team culture based on company values

The Reverse Feedback Session

I always planned in a reverse feedback session in staff members regular 1:1s. You can also setup dedicated sessions.

Here are some rules and pointers about what should (and what should not) happen in the session:

- Always ask them to provide an example if possible. It's easy for anyone to say "you don't delegate enough" without any evidence or example, so some anecdotal samples are very important to substantiate.

- Don't react emotionally to anything that is said. If you have been told of something that you don't like, then don't react immediately. You need to be able to objectively assess the point after the session. The person may be wrong or have simply misunderstood what your intentions were at the time.

- Long term damage could result if you are reactionary in your behaviour. Remain calm and objective. Never get into a war of words.

- Always promise to respond after the session (and make sure you do as you will lose trust if you fail to respond).

- You will probably hear a lot of "everything is fine" or "I can't think of anything to say". The simple tactic here is to pick one of the topics and ask if they can think of a time when you could have done better in that particular area.

- If anyone strays into the personal – i.e. criticises your music taste or choice of comedy ties, then you have to reiterate that the feedback has to remain professional and about your managerial prowess. However, comedy ties aren't funny – upgrade to comedy jumpers or even comedy crocheted jumpers.

Assessing the Feedback

Is what you have heard genuine? Possibly, but you need to make a judgment objectively, so here are some observations:

- Don't take every criticism as accurate. Sometimes employees are having a bad day or are annoyed at something (no bonus this year) and can provide feedback with evidence that is bias to their own perspective. Ask yourself, did you act fairly? Is the criticism a true reflection of what actually happened? It is entirely possible that if you ask other team members you will receive different viewpoints, so who was right? Don't admit anything during the feedback meeting. Say that you will take everything on board and come back to the person. Hearing a criticism can be irritating but you need to remain objective and cool, so you don't have to respond or come up with solutions in the meeting – do it afterwards, but make sure you do otherwise your staff won't trust you.

- I have received feedback that I sometimes wasn't bossy enough – in other words I didn't come down hard enough on people not following processes. This may have been true, but the actual root cause of the issue was one employee having a problem with another employee not following processes. I took it on board though and sent out an email that ALL staff must follow written processes. So sometimes, the solution may not require a change of behaviour from you.

- If, after analysis, there is something you could have done better, then admit it and inform the person who raised the point. I went further and informed the whole group, thanking the person for raising the subject.

Template To Use

Reverse Feedback Topic List

STEP 24 - DIFFICULT CONVERSATIONS MADE EASIER

So, Mable's crocheting needs improving – too many dropped stitches and her whipstitch seams are too loose. Not a difficult conversation that most managers will face, but the topic is irrelevant, it's the techniques that count. There are numerous common practices that all too many managers adopt when a difficult conversation is due:

- They run away from it

- They don't prepare

- They don't listen

- They switch straight into solution mode

- They get side-tracked

- They don't set actions and/or follow up

You cannot afford to ignore the problem. A stitch in time saves nine (especially for crocheters). The issue will grow if you don't face up to it.

I will suggest a process for the conversation and then follow it up with some things you should remember throughout.

The Process

Have Your Template Ready. If you have a memory like mine, then you need to write down what is said during the meeting. There is nothing worse than promising to deliver something and then forgetting. You template should include the following and the conversation flows top to bottom in this order:

- Yours and the employee's names

- The Date

- The Issue or Problem

- The desired outcome

- The employees side of the story

- Actions and Dates

Book a Meeting Room. To ensure privacy, book a meeting room. Trust is a vital ingredient between a manger and his/her staff and one way to build trust is to guarantee their privacy in private discussions. This privacy must be sustained after the meeting, so never discuss anything about this meeting with other staff.

Prepare In Advance. Based on what you know about the issue, what outcome would you like? It is wise to be firm but flexible about the outcome. After you have heard your employees' account, you may have to revise the outcome but be careful not to be managed by the employee – they may employ various diversionary tactics.

Listen. Probably the most important element of the discussion. Are you sure your facts are right? Do you know all the background? What extenuating circumstances are there? Once, on a management training course, we were given the task of having a conversation with someone whose productivity had gone down. Unknown to us, was the fact that this person was having marital difficulties (hypothetically of course). Out of a group of 80+ managers, I was the only one to recognise this fact. I'm not trying to blow my own trumpet here (much easier than blowing someone else's), the point I am making is that nobody else recognised it because they didn't listen or probe enough. It is imperative you hear your staff member's side of the story – you may have been misinformed. While they talk, say nothing and make notes. They will occasionally pause – do NOT be tempted to jump in and fill the gap – let them speak because they will either bring up something new and important or start to get their story crossed, which will help you validate the reality. Executed properly, it is during this phase that you should learn of mitigating circumstances that may be of a very personal nature (but don't push too hard – most people have happy married lives and don't have money worries – they are just lazy sods who need to work harder!!)

Repeat Their Story Back to Them. Paraphrase what they have said and end by saying "Is that right?" If it's not right, then make corrections and then ask again. Their agreement affectively closes off other avenues of conversation (dead ends) and helps you both to zero in on an action.

Collaborate on a Solution. Show your employee that you want to help in solving the problem, but the solution should be a joint effort. Statement such as "How can I help to....", "How can we change how we do it in the department to help?", "Would you like some independent help with this?" show that you are willing to be involved. The employee needs to buy into the solution, so they have to contribute towards the action too. Agree with them how they can do things differently in the future, based on the help you have offered.

Setup and Review some Actions. Clearly, if you arrange a meeting with a staff member, raise a sensitive subject and then do nothing about it afterwards will make your staff think you are "just having a go". Set a maximum of 3 actions and a date for review in the future. Ensure your goals and dates are relevant and achievable. If you ask someone to quadruple their productivity by this time next week, they are going to fail, and this reflects badly on you. It is likely that some of the actions will be yours due to new information you have received. Make sure you deliver on your side of the bargain – "those who live in glass houses" and all that!

Quick Summary. Very briefly run through the actions and dates again and get a verbal agreement from the employee. This rehearses the actions in the employees' mind.

Give the Employee a Copy of the Template. Photocopy or scan and email the template to the employee. Inevitably they will be thinking about the conversation for the next few days or weeks – the document gives them something to refer to in assisting with the completion of their actions. Not that you should feel the need to do this often, but in this case, this action also covers your ass!!

Points to Remember

Be objective. Ensure that your secret favouritisms are not being displayed – you have to assess the situation fairly.

Address the Issue and Not the Person. Focus in on the work-related problem and not the person themselves. Clearly, some issues will be related to interpersonal skills (or a lack of them) so it is more difficult to separate the person from the problem. In these instances, you have to maintain the spotlight on the specific issue and not wander off into other personal issues with the person. I.e. Fred may be generally grumpy, which has led to a customer complaint. Focus on the complaint only and NOT on Fred's general grumpiness. If his sullen attitude manifests into other issues, then deal with these as separate conversations. I know this is more work, but it is all grist to your mill. This approach will help you to highlight to Fred that his general crankiness causes widespread drawbacks. Fred may have an epiphany after a number of difficult conversations and change his persona (but don't hold your breath – it's very difficult to change someone's core characteristics).

The Power of Silence. To say nothing during a very pregnant pause is undoubtedly once of the most uncomfortable acts at work. This is particularly painful for extroverted chatterbox budding thespians, but used correctly, can be a very powerful tool in determining the facts. Striking the appropriate balance is the difficult aspect here. If you ask someone a question that only requires a simple answer, then you can't sit in silence expecting them to say something else. "Do you take milk in your tea?" or "Did you attend the meeting yesterday" only requires "Yes" or "No" answer. Your silences have to be commensurate to the question you are asking. I once had a difficult conversation with my boss over the phone. I had stated my case and wanted to know her reaction, so I said nothing. The silence lasted for an excruciating 2 minutes, but ultimately it worked because she spoke next, and the tone was placatory. So be warned – the employee can use the power of silence too!

Preserve Your Relationship. You work hard, jump through hoops; read articles on Linked In and buy management books (Oh…Hello!) to build relations with your staff – don't destroy them in one conversation. Even if you adopt all the techniques you read in an excellent management book (Hello again!) your employee is likely to view the conversation as a criticism. You will need to adopt your full arsenal of management techniques to preserve your bond. Be helpful, calm, subjective, clear minded, empathic, positive.

Be wary of Dead Ends. Nobody needs debating training in using diversionary tactics to steer a conversation to new (and unhelpful) places – it is instinctive. You can expect your employee to talk around the issue, to deviate into pastures new. Examples of this are to blame others, to say nothing, to talk about other issues or factors. You need to develop your skill at identifying the dead ends (it's a sign in the shape of a T). You have to ask yourself one question "Does this bear any relevance to the issue you are discussing?" If the answer is no, then you need to reaffirm that this discussion is about the issue in question and the conversation will stick to that.

Good Luck, I don't envy you. Right, I'm going to talk to Mable about tightening her whipstitch seams – my bodywork is showing!

Template To Use

Difficult Discussion Template

STEP 25 - TROUBLESOME STAFF

Dump them!

STEP 25 - STILL GOT TROUBLESOME STAFF?

Ok, it's not as simple as just dumping them.

Difficult staff can give you the needle and it's not easy to get off the hook (2 weak wordplays in one sentence. Do 2 weak puns equal 1 good one, or is it just 2 bad puns?)

But seriously, they are the biggest drain on team dynamic; productivity; efficiency and customer relations. No team, regardless of size, should suffer the fallout from one bad penny, but the impact follows an inverse square rule. The smaller the team, the bigger the impact. In short – you frankly cannot have a disrupter in the team.

Technical incompetence can be easily addressed, especially with online training – the Internet makes it easy. It is so simple to find certifications and/or professional qualifications courses and the cost is minimal. There are 1000's of tutoring videos on Youtube that cost nothing – all you have to do is pay for the exam!

On the flip side (there is the inverse rule again), undoing years of upbringing; social input and natural tendencies is extremely difficult, if not impossible. So, trying to change a leopard's spots is going to be challenging and time consuming and you may find at the end of all this effort that the person's intuitive predispositions run through them like the writing in a stick of Blackpool rock. Is it worth risking the time and money for no potential gain? There is no hard and fast answer to this – it may require a judgment call from you. I am an optimist and I believe people should be given a second chance and they do have the ability to change (to a certain degree). I would commit to an initial meeting, at the least and then make a decision based on the employee's reaction.

The Initial Meeting

You will be entering into a difficult conversation, so see the chapter on that to see how to conduct this meeting.

Before you initiate the process however, ask yourself if there really is a problem. Have you got a bee in your bonnet about someone? Are you sure you are unbiased? One negative incident doth not a person make. What does the trend show? Do you have documented evidence? Are you entirely convinced that you are right, and can you back up your convictions?

If you are convinced that there is a real problem, then 2 things:

1. Only tackle one problem at a time. If there is more than one problem, then you will have to address these later after the person has had a chance to solve the first issue. Even if the person has problems, it is unfair and unprofessional for you to hit them with a catalogue of issues simultaneously. If you do this, it will appear to be "personal" so the validity of your accusations will be massively diminished. How can a person be expected to change a number of behaviours at once? If someone is non-communicative and rude, then tackle each separately. Prioritise which to take on first based on the impact of each negative conduct and how easy is it to solve? Certainly engage with any issue that has a large adverse effect, but is easy to solve, first. Problems with small impact and that are difficult to solve, should be prioritised last or not undertaken at all.

2. Evidence. You cannot bring up a subject and then have no evidence to back it up. Anecdotal examples are very worthy in this respect. If you are saying there is a trend, then you should be able to give more than one example, otherwise your allegation looks unfounded.

In the meeting:

- Provide them with a job description which should define job responsibilities and desired behaviours.

- Clearly state what the problem is and what change in behaviour is required.

- What support can you offer? Maybe some form of training (or even counselling) can help – offer this and ensure you deliver.

- Set a deadline. Setup a review sometime in the future, clearly affirming that there needs to be a positive trend leading up to the review. In other words, your employee cannot continue to be an uncooperative, sullen, general pain in the ass but suddenly become an angel for the review.

- What are the consequences? The employee may decide to carry on as before – testing your resolve, so you need to be prepared to outline the consequences if there are no changes forthcoming.

The Review

By initiating the process, you have signed yourself up for a surveillance role. Without being pervasive, monitor the person and make notes of general behaviours. You cannot afford to go into the review unprepared.

- Did you deliver on your promise for support?

- Has the person progressed somewhat but there is still room for improvement? This is progression, but is it enough and fast enough? Only you can answer this – if you believe so then congratulate them on the changes but more work still needs to be done. In this scenario, a 2nd "bite at the apple" seems fair, so a further review is required later on.

The first step in accepting a problem is recognising that it exists. How has the employee reacted? Did they take on board your claims or have they resolutely stuck to their old (bad) ways. If there appears to be recalcitrance and an unwillingness to accept, then you have to decide if you and the company can afford to keep investing in this person.

Experience has shown me that most people will need to be reminded of their weaknesses at least twice to take them seriously, so a second attempt to improve is common. If, by the 2nd review, the situation has not improved, then you are probably "flogging a dead horse" and it's time to unleash your consequences!

The Consequences

If after the 2nd review, grumpy Joe remains "grumpy" then you should involve HR. Indeed, I would go further and state that HR should drive the process from now on. There are many employment rules, so leave it to the professionals. Your company or organisation will have it's own procedures for this, which usually follows the pattern of:

1. One or two verbal warnings

2. One or two written warnings

3. Sacking or compromise agreement.

There could be an occasion when someone fulfils all their job role duties, so legally cannot be sacked, however, their conduct is a negative influence on your team. In this scenario, you could end up offering a compromise agreement which will depend on your company's policy. It is your job to describe the magnitude of the negative impact resulting from the person's behaviour to assist HR in deciding on the size of the pay out in the compromise agreement.

Contractors are easier to get rid of because they don't have any employment rights. I've done this a number of times with contractors who were expensive and didn't deliver.

In short, you absolutely cannot have a fly in your ointment, so get

STEP 25 - STILL GOT TROUBLESOME STAFF?

swatting. The process is difficult and not very enjoyable, but you have to think of the bigger picture. It's like cutting out a cancer to ensure the body survives. Give people a chance and support them, but it is very challenging to change someone's core personality and (unfortunately) most of the time you will.........erm.........dump them!

MANAGER'S DASHBOARD

To be a data overlord – Create a good dashboard

Aside from a good template (and of course a well hooked crochet blanket, which incidentally is referred to as an Afghan), the next best thing is a dashboard. I should get out more.

How well are you doing? You have all these disparate ratings which should be giving you some pointers of your performance. Pulling them together into the Manager's Dashboard will provide an overall rating of how you are doing.

In the supplied dashboard, you can only get a proper rating at the end of the year as the dashboard requires you to answer some questions about progress of certain areas looking back. If you complete it mid-year, you will get some strange results as the dashboard will show that you have only part completed some scheduled things.

Some of the dashboard elements are calculated and are based on the number of people in your team. For example – there should be 4 quarterly plans for each person, so for a team of 8 people, there would be 32 quarterly plans. Thus, the first entry you complete on the dashboard is the number of people in your team.

Below are listed the components of the dashboard along with any calculated ratings and the assumptions the calculation uses:

- For the KPIs defined for your department, what percentage have hit target or above?

- What is the average % of completion for the goals/projects you set? You can pull this from your department goals progress.

- How many quarterly plans were set in the year? (The calculation uses 4 quarterly plans per person per year)

- What is the average % of completion for the quarterly plans you set? You can pull this from your quarterly plans overview.

- What % of the department meetings that you scheduled have been held. I.e. have any department meetings been missed or not held?

- What percentage of staff still remain out of the total number that have been employed in your team? This is measuring your staff retention.

- How many 1:1s in total were scheduled in the year? (The calculation assumes one 1:1 per person per month).

- Of the 1:1s you have scheduled, what % that have been held. I.e. have any 1:1s been missed or not held?

- How many coaching sessions have been held in the year? (The calculation assumes one coaching sessions per person per year).

- How many courses/certifications or other development plans did you schedule in the year? (The calculation assumes 2 courses/certifications per person per year).

- Of the courses/certifications/developments that you planned, what percentage have been completed? You can get this from your training progress spreadsheet.

- How many job swaps were scheduled in the year? (The calculation assumes 2 job swaps per person per year)

- Of the job swaps you planned, what percentage have been completed? You can get this from the Job Swapping Spreadsheet.

- The difference between the biggest and smallest workload as a percentage of the average workload. You can pull this from your workload calculator.

- For the number of different roles your department has, what percentage of them have job descriptions defined?

- What percentage of the planned yearly appraisals have been completed?

- What is your overall delegation rating? You can get this from your delegation rating spreadsheet.

- What is your average score from the 360° review? If there was no 360° review, put 0.

- What is your overall percentage rating from the Employee Survey? Get this from the Employee Survey if you have one. If not, put 0.

The Dashboard will then calculate your average score of all the above ratings to show your overall performance. You can copy the tabs to record your performance for each year and see if the general trend is up (which it should be). I can be seen on Thursday nights peering into cars satisfying my dashboard fetish.

Template To Use

Managers Dashboard

MICRO MANAGER OR DISENGAGED STAR GAZER?

In 1890, when I was a mere 25 years old, I underwent one of the most embarrassing and frustrating encounters with my micro manager boss. I was an analyst programmer and regularly worked an extra 40-60 minutes every day outside of normal office hours. One day I was about 10 minutes late due to the wrong type of leaves on the road and he asked me into his room to discuss why I was late. I can remember wanting to lean across his desk and give him a good shake (and that's the PC version – the real version involved teeth and throat!). I left that meeting feeling demeaned, embarrassed, frustrated, annoyed and, most importantly, demotivated for the rest of the day. All my efforts to mature as an individual and show commitment to work evaporated because I now felt like a scolded child. I vowed from that day that, if I were to end up as a manager, I would treat my staff as grown-ups with respect.

Unfortunately, I have encountered other micro managers since (which does raise the point that I may be the root cause!).

Here are some of the behaviours of micro managers that I have witnessed:

- Attending all the low level (detail) meetings of their staff

- Constant checking of staff output

- Ensuring that all communication goes through them, especially to other superiors in the organisation

- Cannot delegate

- A general inability to empower staff to get on with their job

- An overall failure to treat people as adults and with respect

- Tends to be (or at least gives the impression of being) a perfectionist

The resulting culture is negative and reduces productivity due to

- A closed relationship between manager and staff

- Creativity is stifled because staff are wary of the reaction they will get to new suggestion

- The department can become very bureaucratic and obsessed by adherence to processes

- Employees feel they are constantly being judged so "clam up" reducing internal communication

- People don't "own" their work, as the ultimate accountability will reside with the boss

- The department becomes stale and can develop an "us and them" ethos where rumours are rife.

There is always a Yang to a Ying, so what's the opposite of a micro manager? I call them disengaged star gazers because they spend a lot of time looking outwards (mainly upwards) from the department, giving an impression they are disengaged and uninterested in the daily machinations of department life. I have encountered these too and although the symptoms are very different, one key net result is the same – productivity goes down.

Here are the star gazer symptoms

- Is commonly bored with daily operations

- Don't conduct meaningful 1:1s with staff (or don't do 1:1s at all

- Don't organise regular department meetings (too boring!

- Do provide news from above. This shows they are more in touch with what's happening in the business

- Network with superiors in the organisation. It is common for star gazers to also be promotion hunters

- Rarely provides meaningful appraisals or development plans for staff

- Don't stay long in the job

- Radiate an aura of "looking after No. 1" and usually this is true.

So, the upshot is

- An unstructured and unfocused department – a lot of chatting goes on.

- Staff are unsure of theirs and the departments goal

- Employees are stressed by upcoming appraisals because they know the boss has been out of touch for previous 12 months – "he doesn't know what I have achieved".

- Staff regularly discuss who the next boss is going to be

- Disorganised work practises and processes

The star gazer departments are usually happier than micro managed ones because they are not being scrutinised. However, the star gazer departments are typically less productive as they have no set targets or goals.

As in life "a bit of everything in moderation" is the soundest approach.

Set out a charter for the department to cover the expected behaviours of the manager and staff

- Write down your responsibilities to be a good manager. (Just writing it down will, or should, drive you towards delivering on the promises.) I won't micro manage. I will provide regular feedback. I will conduct regular 1:1s. I will work towards staff development. I will set targets and review them. I will keep staff informed of company news.

- Brainstorming sessions will be held where everyone is expected to contribute. (Your first brainstorming session can be the development of this charter. You will be amazed how innovative people are even with seemingly boring or trivial tasks).

- Staff are expected to deal with personal differences in a mature, courteous and professional manner.

- Staff are expected to take accountability for their tasks without interruption from the manager.

- Generate some general communication guidelines for internal and external purposes.

- Staff are expected to contribute in a positively professional manner

- Your door is always open (if you have one!)

There is probably much more subject matter that you can think of to be in the charter – just be careful it doesn't become too big and unwieldy because, as with any agreement or process, it has to be revisited regularly to ensure everyone understands and abides by it. It should be a living document so don't think that once it is created you can forget it. You also need to "walk the talk" and ensure you live up to your side of the bargain – if you do, then your staff will deliver too.

HOW APPROACHABLE IS YOUR DEPARTMENT?

The following is all based on an IT department because they always say one should write about what they know. The concept, though, can be applied to any department, especially those that provide a service to other departments within an organisation.

Having worked in SMEs and large corporations, I have witnessed different outcomes from the "Approachability of IT". SMEs tend to have a "door is always open" policy whereas large corporations metaphorically lock the door from the inside; install pressure pads and laser detection devices to warn of incoming users. Getting the balance right can have dramatic and positive results on the user perception of your department and reduces stress in IT employees.

It would be lovely to have a completely "open door" policy with coffee and biscuits (and perhaps some communal quilt sewing if you are so inclined) but herein lies chaos. Without any rules on how to approach IT (including the raising of service tickets), you end up with a system of "he who shouts the loudest, gets served first".

I have actually witnessed IT Support in large corporations physically locking the department door to stop users wandering in. Calling people "users" is wrong to begin with – it promotes negative stereotypes – loan sharks spring to mind. We should use the word "customers" as the first step to facing the IT department outwards with an ingrained service mentality.

Clearly the best approach is a compromise of the two cultures. We can have an open door, but with some clearly laid out rules on approaching IT.

Most larger companies will have their Servicedesk procedures sorted – i.e. many ways of raising service tickets, usually by phone, email or intranet page. These rules are ok for 95% of the time, but what about emergency situations? What if production is stopped due to an IT issue? The IT approach rules should describe what the process should be in an emergency situation. My take on it is that IT's door is wide open (with a red carpet) for these situations. Sort the problem out first and do the paperwork afterwards.

Generally in life, VIPs get to bend the rules, so let them bend the IT rules a bit. There is nothing worse for the perception of the IT department (and also your promotion prospects) than a "job's worth" IT supporter asking a VIP "Have you raised a service ticket?" VIPs perception of the whole IT provision is based on the personal service they receive, so a 30 second conversation between an overzealous IT supporter and a VIP can damage all the work you do for the rest of the year.

Write your "Approaching IT" rules. They should define the normal process (i.e. raising service tickets etc.), what to do in an emergency situation and treatment for VIPS. Now you have to broadcast – there is no point in having the rules if nobody knows about them. Customers and your IT staff have to understand the rules properly, so make sure there are no excuses for not knowing them. Email them to all customers, put it on your intranet page, and (very importantly), print a copy on A3 and stick it to the IT department's door.

Finally, you have to stand up for your staff. There will always be troublemakers who believe the rules don't apply to them (non VIPs I mean). Assuming your staff remain professional, courteous and are abiding by the rules, then they need to know what to do with the rule breakers. Tempting though it is, you cannot have a trap door to a deep pit, so the Approach rules must define what your staff do in these cases. All customers will get to see this and so should reduce the number of unwelcome visits!

When implemented correctly, it is amazing how IT staff behaviours change. Knowing they have a clearly defined set of rules, that the customers know too, promotes a healthier mood – you definitely hear less moaning "Oh god, not him again. That's the third time this week". Indeed, relationships between IT staff and customers tends to improve and become more social, which helps with integrating IT into the business.

A LIST OF THE TEMPLATES

All these templates can be downloaded by visiting this address on the internet: www.duncanjandrews.co.uk

Behaviour Rating Survey and Applicants Appraisal

Responsibilities

Job Description Template

1:1 Template

Yearly Appraisal Template

Department Meeting Template

Delegation Rating

Smart Goals Template

Training Progress

Coaching Template

Converting Strategic Goals into Actions

Brainstorming Ideas Evaluation

Quarterly Plans Overview and Quarterly Plan Template

Task to Skills Template

Skills Matrix Template

Job Swapping Template

360 Review Template

Workloads Calculator

Reverse Feedback Topic List

Managers Dashboard

Difficult Discussion Template

Project or Task Evaluation Tool

Departmental Goals Progress

Templates

All of them!!!

Printed in Great Britain
by Amazon